The rise and fall of a profession?

Steve Rogowski

First published in Great Britain in 2010 by

The Policy Press
University of Bristol
Fourth Floor
Beacon House
Queen's Road
Bristol BS8 1QU
UK

t: +44 (0)117 331 4054
f: +44 (0)117 331 4093
tpp-info@bristol.ac.uk
www.policypress.co.uk

North American office:
The Policy Press
c/o International Specialized Books Services (ISBS)
920 NE 58th Avenue, Suite 300
Portland, OR 97213-3786, USA
t: +1 503 287 3093
f: +1 503 280 8832
info@isbs.com

British Library Cataloguing in Publication Data
A catalogue record for this book is available from the British Library.

Library of Congress Cataloging-in-Publication Data
A catalog record for this book has been requested.

ISBN 978 1 84742 448 8 paperback

Cover design by The Policy Press
Front cover: photograph kindly supplied by Fernando Rico
Printed and bound in Great Britain by Hobbs, Southampton
The Policy Press uses environmentally responsible print partners

Let's drink to the hard working people
Let's drink to the lowly at birth
Raise your glass to the good and the evil
Let's drink to the salt of the earth.

The Rolling Stones, 'Salt of the Earth', 1968

Contents

Foreword

> But science is also now continually reshaping its history retrospectively. It is starting to look back and rediscover its beginnings, its earlier traditions and triumphs; but also its debates, its uncertainties and its errors. (Holmes, 2008, p 468)

As with science, so it is with social work. And as with science, social work is also a creature of its times. The ideological, political, social and economic contemporary contexts are all influences on the positioning of social work and the roles it plays. But this is not the total story. Individuals sometimes swim against the contemporary tides with a vision of what should be and how things could be different, and sometimes they have an impact. This was the achievement, for example, of the social reformers and social researchers of the 19th century, challenging poverty and destitution and the negative impact of the Poor Law. It could be so today with resistance to punitive government policies towards young people, asylum seekers and people with mental health difficulties, who are demonised by politicians and by a press that is allowed to have so much power.

But a question is how to have a positive impact when swimming against the contemporary current? Praxis, with practical knowledge applied to action, should be a golden thread running through all that we do as social workers with principles, politics and pragmatism all playing a part in shaping practice. But note that it is principle that comes first; the politics and pragmatism are about how best to seek impact but the principles define what is to be achieved.

Within social work it is the value base that should underpin all that we do. It is about challenging discrimination and tackling disadvantage and deprivation, and about valuing people and recognising their contribution and capacity as well as their problems and maybe the difficulties they create for others.

And it is often analysis and then anger that drives action, with an outrage about how some are left marginalised, stranded and victimised within an overall context of affluence and opportunity. Those with position and economic power dominate, even when their behaviour is exposed as immoral, as with the get-rich-quick, self-interested bankers of the late 2000s. They ride the storm with their media contacts and control, soon turning the story back to a script about scroungers on benefits, 'foreigners taking our jobs' and incompetent public sector workers.

This is the reality for social work and social workers working alongside people who are marginalised but within a reality largely defined and described by the rich and powerful. It is not a comfortable or confident position, with abuse and vilification turned on social workers themselves when a child dies in horrific circumstances that in themselves are often the result of ingrained disadvantage for generations of families and communities.

This book by Steve Rogowski has a subterranean current of anger flowing through it, an anger based on experience and knowledge gained while staying close as a social work practitioner to the disadvantage and distress of those with whom he has worked for over 35 years. It is a study rooted in political science and philosophy, and economic and social theory, all with a platform provided by Marxism. The analysis is about power and the impact on people. It is well informed and insightful, being a book for close reading not browsing, with a current of argument to be absorbed. Only dipping the toe into the intellectual sea of ideas from page to page will miss the ebb and flow of what has happened to social work over the years. But the effort of reading rather than browsing this book is not overly challenging. The volume has depth and breadth, is readable and relevant, and is erudite and explanatory. It is riveting and realistic.

By the end of the book, like Rogowski, I was enthused and energised to make a contribution within social work so that social work itself can make a positive contribution to society. The messages I took away with me were that social workers should collectively seek to create a stronger voice to champion social work's principles and value base, and that this is best achieved by building a stronger professional identity and professional organisation, with this profession to be about sharing experience and expertise with service users, about being allies alongside them and the collective and organised voices service users have created.

As well as the message about acting collectively, there is the potential impact of individual action. Social work is often given little political attention. This can feel as though social work is being neglected and ignored, but there is also a possibility here to act below the political radar. The 1989 Children Act, with its focus in part on working in partnership with parents where families were in difficulty, was hardly within the mainstream of Thatcherite ideology, but it was driven forward with little political debate by a small number of civil servants and judges informed by academic researchers.

In addition, what we know from research about the views of service users is that the social worker's behaviour has particular importance. Are they reliable, considerate, trustworthy, open and honest? It may be that for people who are often denigrated and damaged by their contacts with others, the positive experience of the relationship with social workers has particular meaning. But on reflection, this is so for us all, service users and social workers. We each and all value the positive relationships in our lives. This book is rooted in an analysis of power but within a concern throughout for people. Just like social work itself.

Ray Jones, June 2010

Ray Jones is professor of social work at Kingston University and St George's, University of London. He is also a registered social worker and was formerly director of social services in Wiltshire and chair of the British Association of Social Workers.

Acknowledgements

The first people to acknowledge are those children, young people, families, individuals and communities with whom I have tried to make a positive difference.

Alan Bartlett encouraged and helped in the very early stages of my entry to social work. Others I need to mention are from my social work student days, notably lecturers/tutors David Thorpe, David Smith and Peter Beresford, as well as fellow students. Over the years other academics such as Audrey Mullender and Beth Humphries have played a part.

As a practitioner, there are many people I could mention (as well as many people I would not want to). Dave Boardman and Mark Limmer were committed community workers, and Maureen McGrath was a progressive health visitor. Betty Holden was an inspirational welfare rights activist. Councillor Margaret Riley had an understanding, and was therefore a supporter, of social work. Senior colleagues like Gwen Swire, Bob Lewis and, later, Linda Priest were all committed to social work and its values, and tried to ensure that their staff had the opportunity to do their job as it should be done. Then there is a range of practitioners and administrative/clerical staff (the latter generally not considering themselves as 'business support' workers), only a few of whom can be named here – John Mullis, Ann Tunnicliffe, Martin Richardson, David Wood, Denis Heyes, Cath Coombes, Pam Jones, Leza Harrison, Jim Murphy, Gill Adams and Gill Silversides. Some of these people have passed away and others have retired, but, one way or another, they have all been a friendly and supportive influence. These latter comments apply to many current colleagues, even though they are often preoccupied with bureaucracy being completed and processed as speedily as possible – they know who they are. Finally, there are family and friends, who, while they were always probably wondering what I was up to, have managed to stay interested. Apologies to anyone I have missed out.

ONE

Introduction: the rise and fall of social work?

In March 2008, I attended a conference entitled 'Affirming our Value Base in Social Work and Social Care' held at Nottingham Trent University. It was a follow-up to a similar one I had attended there in 2006 and, as previously, it turned out to be an exhilarating day. There were contributions from well-known academics such as Lena Dominelli, Iain Ferguson and Peter Beresford, as well as service users[1] and practitioners. There was considerable concern about the direction social work has been forced to take over recent years, leading to a deprofessionalisation of the role largely because of the growth and influence of managerialism. One result is increased bureaucracy, which often means intrusively gathering information so that forms and computer exemplars can be filled in. Then there are the performance targets, which are meaningless as far as most users and practitioners are concerned. Despite all this, most people left the conference with renewed confidence and optimism for the future of social work.

Peter Beresford reminded everyone that Daphne Statham, the former stalwart of the National Institute of Social Work, once said that it is still possible to 'smuggle in' good practice despite managerial obstacles. One can still build relationships with users, work with them at their pace on problems and difficulties as defined by them, treat them with dignity and respect, be non-judgemental and so on. All this is not to minimise the very real difficulties that practitioners face on a daily basis.

Resisting what has and is currently happening to social work is certainly a difficult task, but again the conference highlighted some possibilities. Social workers could come together and form social work action groups to voice their concerns. For example, there is the Social Work Action Network, a loose coalition of workers, academics

1

and service users that organises conferences on issues such as social work and asylum seekers, the demonisation of young people and the impact of managerialism (see Ferguson and Woodward, 2009). Social workers can also build alliances with user groups and councillors, again pointing out their disquiet together with suggestions for possible ways forward. Being active within, and putting pressure on, the British Association of Social Workers (BASW) is another avenue to pursue. And as an individual practitioner, sometimes it is still possible to make a difference. Sadly, however, the renewed vigour and enthusiasm the conference engendered was soon to be dented.

On returning to the office, I immediately reported to colleagues about the day and received some positives replies from social workers. A senior manager with many years of practice experience agreed with my overall sentiments, but remained pessimistic about the general future of social work. However, what was more disconcerting were comments made by two other managers. One simply queried why I had been paid to attend the conference because my views were 'so anti-management'. Another had similar views, even intimating that I should not have reported back from the day, this despite the fact that after attending training events it is custom and practice to do precisely this for the benefit of colleagues. I was also asked to call in and see this particular manager 'for a chat when you have got a spare minute or two'. Unsurprisingly, largely because of time spent filling in forms/exemplars, I never got round to it. Perhaps I should have made more of an effort, as a lively discussion would doubtless have ensued.

Not long afterwards, I spent two days on the Integrated Children's System (ICS)[2] computer course followed by two days on office duty. This meant I was only able to spend one day that week actually seeing and working with the service users on my caseload. At about the same time, Hall et al (2008) reported on their research into information and communication technologies (ICT). They pointed out that ICT, along with performance management, have become central to how social work is practised, and it is fanciful to presume that they can be separated as if they were an ancillary task. On occasions, this means social workers spend 80% of their time on the computer rather than spending time with the people they are supposed to be helping.

A little later, I took a referral from a housing officer that concerned a young, lone, depressed mother who was having difficulties with her five-year-old son. Typically, he had temper tantrums and would not do as he was told, and neighbours complained about his 'antisocial behaviour', which included throwing stones at them as well as passers-by. He had been excluded from school in the past because of his poor behaviour, including 'hitting' his head teacher. There was also a suggestion that he was suffering from attention deficit hyperactivity disorder (ADHD). My initial thoughts envisaged a social worker engaging with the family, getting to know them, discussing the issues and concerns, and jointly working out ways forward. It would have at least involved an initial assessment. A team manager, though, thought differently. If the housing officer met with the family, together with representatives from the school and the health service, they could, utilising the Common Assessment Framework (CAF)[3], look at the issues and work out ways forward. This could have involved referral to the National Children's Home (now Action for Children) for work on parenting, and the local child mental health unit regarding ADHD. There was no role, the argument went, for social work. As a colleague remarked in more colloquial terms, this amounted to 'fobbing people off' by asking them to fill in a form. Moreover, she went on, such an attitude applied not just to fellow professionals but even to users when they contacted the office for assistance. Aspects of this scenario reinforce the view that facets of what once amounted to social work are now being undertaken by other 'professionals'.

There were two other developments. First, I came across *Making it Happen* (DCSF, 2008). This document refers to the help and support that can be provided to children and young people by an array of workers, including learning mentors, support workers, health visitors and teachers. However, like former BASW chair and director of social services, and now professor, Ray Jones (2008), I was struck by the fact that there was not one mention of social work or social workers. Like him, one wonders why the fact that thousands of children and families receive advice, assistance and, when necessary, protective action was not acknowledged or recognised by a New Labour government. And second, there was the publication of *Social Work at its Best: a statement of social work roles and tasks for the 21st century*

(General Social Care Council, 2008). This document had been lying on ministers' desks for months before it was sneaked out without a formal launch, press release or ministerial forward. Furthermore, although it refers to values embodying equality and human rights and the profession being committed to enabling all to meet their potential, there are also statements about social workers being brokers, navigators and planners. These latter comments are reminiscent of words used to introduce care management for adult service users in the 1990s, something that in many ways was the forerunner to current changes in relation to social work with children and families.

In short, after a rejuvenating conference, plus the publication of an optimistic, or some might say utopian, article about the possibilities of a radical/critical practice (Rogowski, 2008), I was quickly back to the reality of what so-called social work now comprises, together with the esteem with which New Labour held it. Although social work has been probably the most disparaged and discredited profession of the past 35 years, this intensified under New Labour. Managerialism, marketisation and scapegoating by the media and politicians certainly appear to have contributed to widespread demoralisation (Jones, 1999, 2004). I have long bemoaned the changes that have taken place in social work over the years (for example, Rogowski, 2002, 2007) but had always managed to retain a sense of optimism for the future. But after years of, in a professional sense, swimming against the tide, perhaps it was time to take stock. Some refer to the 'remaking' and 'transforming' of social work (Garrett, 2003 and 2009b respectively), the 'repositioning' of social work (Dominelli, 2009a) or of social work being subject to 'continuity and change' (Payne, 2005a). However, another view is that what remains of the profession is at best a severely truncated and technocratic version of what it once promised to be. All these changes then, the development of social work to arguably its current nadir, are what this book is about.

Locating myself

Before elaborating on what will be for many a controversial view, I want to say something about the book's antecedents, including my own intellectual and social work biography. The point is that I need to make myself visible, not out of self-indulgence, but as a way of alerting the reader to the obvious fact that I am not all-knowing or impartial and that different interpretations and conclusions about developments in social work can be made. Despite frequent calls for, or claims of, objectivity, we all come to our views based on various assumptions and values, and I want to make mine clear.

I was brought up in a working-class family that had middle-class aspirations and went to Leeds University to study law during the late 1960s/early 1970s. I engaged in some of the student 'sit-ins' of the time, though generally was little interested in politics. Most of my student days were spent socialising, drinking alcohol, listening to and watching rock music, and by and large attempting to have as good a time as possible. On graduating, I was unsure of what I wanted to do and spent some months doing various casual jobs in factories and department stores. I was struck by the boring and mundane nature of the work that many people are forced into, and it was during this period that a more serious interest in politics developed. I had many discussions with friends who had attended what appeared to be more radical universities such as Essex and the London School of Economics. They had studied what I was beginning to see as more interesting subjects such as sociology, politics and economics. I also came across Miliband's (1973) *The State in Capitalist Society*, which provides an analysis of the capitalist system of power.

In 1973, I joined the civil service as an employment adviser in (the then) Department of Employment. I was unsure of what I wanted to do, and being convinced that there were others in the same boat, I thought that I could do something to help. During my discussions with 'claimants', the unemployed, or 'jobseekers' and 'customers' as they are now called, I was struck by the various problems that many were facing. There were those with obvious difficulties, such as physical and mental health issues and learning needs. And then there were those who simply seemed keen to opt out of the system altogether, not wanting to become engaged in traditional employment. Rather they were content to, for example, squat or live in communes in unoccupied property, existing on benefits and anything else they could make money from. They would sell their paintings, home-made jewellery or even 'soft' drugs such as cannabis in order to get by. Some also saw themselves as harbingers of alternative, more egalitarian forms of living. I began to see such views and lifestyles as challenges to conventional, capitalist society.

I was reasonably content in the civil service, but did miss the student lifestyle and the relative freedom and socialising that it brought. Less flippantly, I wanted to do something more in terms of addressing the social problems that I saw on a day-to-day basis as an employment adviser. This is where social work came in and I went on to complete a Diploma in Social Work (which incorporated the Certificate of Qualification in Social Work) at Lancaster University. It was here that I became interested in juvenile delinquency, as young offending was then called, and its community-based management by means of intermediate treatment[4]. Essentially, it came to be about developing alternatives to incarceration for young offenders because of its ineffectiveness in terms of high reconviction rates, and because it was very expensive as well as inhumane (see Thorpe et al, 1980).

My interest in Marx developed with the appearance of my first social work article, which argued that social workers dealt with casualties of a capitalist system that is dominated by profit and property owning rather than the real needs of people (Rogowski, 1977). This was also influenced by other seminal texts, *Radical Social Work* (Bailey and Brake, 1975) and *The New Criminology: for a social theory of deviance* (Taylor et al, 1973). These works point to the fact that paradoxically the justification of social work lies in its maintenance of a social and economic system that is the cause of the ills that it has to confront. In the case of young offenders, for instance, then and now, social work involves ensuring that young people play by the rule of current society without recognising that these rules, and the inequalities of wealth and power involved, lie at the heart of youth crime.

After qualifying as a social worker, my first post was as a generic worker dealing with a range of duties and responsibilities in relation to all service user groups. In addition to individual casework, I was also involved in group and community-oriented work, including establishing a local claimants' union and a lone parents' group. I also had my first taste of working with young offenders by organising and facilitating intermediate treatment groups (see, for example, Rogowski, 1982) along with groups for the parents of offenders. I completed an MA in 1982, the thesis looking at intermediate treatment and the potential for a radical practice, drawing on notions of politicisation and consciencisation (Rogowski, 1985).

In 1983, I became a social worker for children and families, which I have been ever since. I have always been keen to develop a radical social work practice, having been involved in group work with parents who had children on the child protection register and with young people who were solvent users (Rogowski and McGrath, 1986 and Rogowski et al, 1989 respectively; see also Mullender, 1989/90). This work influenced and formed part of attempts at developing community social work strategies on two deprived estates. Such work involved working alongside local people utilising group and community work methods, as well as traditional casework, some of which is discussed further in Chapter Three.

In undertaking a Personal Social Services Fellowship in the late 1980s, I again looked at the possibilities of developing a radical practice for intermediate treatment (see Rogowski, 1990a, 1990b, 1995). By this time, radical social work had changed in that it was not only issues of class that had to be considered but also those of 'race'[5] and gender (Langan and Lee, 1989). All this took place despite the neoliberal onslaught that began with the election of Thatcher in 1979, the collapse of the Soviet Bloc, the subsequent crisis within Marxist thought and the influence of postmodernism. As a result, social work increasingly had to cope with dramatic changes at the economic, political and ideological level, as well as in terms of social theory. A key book that looks at such issues, asking and trying to answer the question 'what has become of social work and what are its futures?' was Parton's (1996a) edited collection *Social Theory, Social Change and Social Work*. It looks at the theory, policy and practice of social work under the Conservative governments of 1979 to the mid-1990s and I make no apologies for drawing on some of the essays in this book.

During the mid-1990s, my thoughts turned to studying for a PhD. I was interested in the policy and practice changes in relation to youth crime over the postwar period – simply put, the move from welfare/ treatment to punishment – and was curious to know what young offenders made of them. My research included a qualitative study that involved semi-structured interviews and focus group discussions with young offenders. It amounted to critical social research, an approach that relates social phenomena to a wider social context as well as challenging oppression (Harvey, 1990).

The young people saw offending as something that started as naughtiness or mischief, 'graduating' to more instrumental offending motivated by boredom and material gain (Rogowski, 2000/01, 2006). They condemned the move from welfare/treatment to punishment, also seeing the youth justice system as racist, sexist and as focusing on young people 'like us' from deprived areas rather than administering justice to all. Young offending, they went on, should be tackled by making school more interesting and relevant, improving recreational facilities and ensuring that there were genuine employment and training opportunities. Parents and carers also needed more support and resources. All this, they argued, would mean young offending was seriously addressed. They were concerned with inequality, feeling that a fairer, more just society would lead to less crime. It was from their views and experiences that I argued for a radical/critical practice (Rogowski 2003/04, 2008) as well as a radical/critical social policy (Rogowski, 2010).

Some of the foregoing may seem rather naive and idealistic, especially when one considers that we are now living in neoliberal or even postmodern times. However, I think the key point to make is that we could live in a better world, one where at the very least there is less inequality and less oppression based on 'race', gender, disability and so on. This is what social work, although initially endeavouring to deal with problems and difficulties confronting people on an individual basis, has to keep in mind. This must involve a critical perspective, one that acknowledges the strength of Marxist theory. Perhaps social class and the capitalist, now more usually termed neoliberal, economic system are not sufficient explanations for inequality and oppression in society (although many would disagree; see, for example, Callinicos, 2001, 2003), with other structural factors including 'race' and gender coming into play and needing to be taken into account. Such a perspective leads to a radical or critical practice that questions dominant ideological assumptions, and aims to understand and change the social and political context of practice (Cree and Myers, 2008). After all, knowledge is structured by existing social relations and these are oppressive in nature, being rooted in the aforementioned differences in relation to class, 'race' and gender and so forth. Recognising this, while perhaps not making the task any easier, means there is an opportunity to do something about it. A more open engagement with issues of power is therefore necessary so as to open up possibilities of negotiation and transformation.

The book: preliminary considerations

Having 'located myself', it is now timely to say something about the book itself. As indicated, it essentially charts the highs and current lows of the development of social work as a profession.

At the outset, a key question is 'what actually is a profession?'. Although there is a considerable literature on this, including that of one of the giants of sociology, Durkheim, actually there is no generally accepted definition other than perhaps a profession has claims to special knowledge and skills that require extensive training (Johnson, 1993). Medicine and law are generally accepted as 'classical' autonomous professions, whereas other occupational groups such as accountants, teachers, nurses and social workers, are best regarded as 'semi' or 'bureau' professions. Nevertheless, one could still argue that during the 1970s social work did contain elements of a genuine profession. There was a period of training with resulting practice based on knowledge, understanding and skills together with an element of autonomy and discretion in how to practice. However, since the 1980s, all this has gradually been eroded as managerialism has increasingly taken hold. What now exists is a so-called professionalism based on organisational rather than professional values emphasising bureaucratic and managerial controls, budgetary restrictions and financial rationalisations, all of which require the standardisation of work practices (Rogowski, 2007). It amounts to the 'deformation of professional formation', with being 'professional' nowadays often merely amounting to delivering someone else's targets (Green, 2009). In making this point, I want to emphasise that I am not defending professional privilege, and the power and prestige this can involve.

Instead, my views are grounded in a set of values and a code of ethics that include ensuring basic human rights and social justice, and, one might add, genuine equality, for all. Such views are, at least potentially, oppositional to neoliberalism and they are ones that explain why many come into social work in the first place.

Developments in social work are in turn related to ideological changes in the economic, political and social spheres. In theorising social welfare and in turn social work's evolution, it is important to link such spheres to wider philosophical and political problematics and, in particular, the debate about Enlightenment philosophy (O'Brien and Penna, 1998). The importance of theory in examining the development of social work cannot be overstated. Social work's history is much more than a series of events to be presented in simple chronological order, letting the facts speak for themselves, as it were. The reason for this is that *all* social and economic policy as well as social and economic research is based on theory at some level or other. There is no such thing as pure, empirically based policy or atheoretical research. Furthermore, theory is not a wordgame carried out by academics. Rather, it is a dimension of action because it gives direction and meaning to what we do, this being another reason why I dealt with my own intellectual and social work biography.

In looking at Enlightenment philosophy and the associated question of modernity, of particular relevance to the beginnings of social work in the middle of the 19th and into the 20th century were liberalism and, later, Marxism. This was when the forerunner of modern social work, the Charity Organisation Society, developed, and when the state, often reluctantly, became more involved in welfare provision. From the middle of the 20th century to the 1970s, when Marxist views were at their height, we see the dominance of the social democratic consensus of the postwar years. This led to the establishment of the welfare state and was the period when social work as a profession reached its zenith. Subsequently, there was the move to the neoliberal consensus of the present, which embraces Thatcherism, Majorism, the Blairism and Brownism of New Labour, and now the Conservative–Liberal Democratic coalition government of David Cameron. One result has been the demise of the welfare state and social work. Paralleling this move, Enlightenment and modernity come under challenge from postmodernism, not least its questioning of science and grand narratives including political philosophies and ideologies. The foregoing needs to be born in mind when considering social work's development.

Enlightenment and modernity

Enlightenment and modernity refer to the changed world view that developed from the 18th century onwards, a key aspect being the belief that by virtue of reason and science, explanation and progress could be achieved for humanity. Modernity sees the major lines of development and change in the contemporary world as being consistent with, or an historical product of, an unfolding pattern of events inaugurated by the social, political, economic and epistemological revelations of Enlightenment (O'Brien and Penna, 1998). This represented a major shift towards scientific and secular explanations of the natural and social world, an important characteristic of which was the separation of 'man' and human 'reason' from the natural order. It was confined to a particular geographical region, largely western Europe, and although commonly understood as a specific historical period, it also refers to a number of intellectual, cultural, social and political developments that opened up the world to the rational autonomous thought of human beings, subjecting the institutions of church, state and law to the power of rational thought. It represented an era in which philosophy understood itself as entering the light of reason from the darkness of myth and superstition.

The rise of scientific and secular philosophical interpretations of nature and society undermined the legitimacy of established world views and opened up space for social, ethical and political relationships to be understood as a result of human action and organised through such action (Touraine, 1995). Enlightenment thinkers were secure in their belief that reason, logic and science could be applied universally – to history, to nature, to the human body and mind, and to society – and that a single philosophical system could be developed within which everything would be revealed to human understanding. There

—

was a faith in science as a progressive force that could understand and solve problems in both the natural and social worlds (Hamilton, 1997).

When it comes to the social world, although the possibilities of Enlightenment were understood in different ways by different thinkers, there was a preoccupation with power and its foundations, what rights individuals could properly lay claim to, and what form of political organisation could guarantee individual rights. All this formed the substance of intense philosophical disputes during the 18th and 19th centuries with a major division existing between philosophers such as Locke, whose work provided important inspiration for liberalism, and those of the French Enlightenment, such as Rousseau, who provided many of the foundations for Marxism. For Locke, free will characterised human activity, and the primary purpose of that activity was labour, so the protection through laws enabling individual freedom to act, trade and own property was the proper role of political authority. Against this was counterposed an alternative understanding of social order based on individual submission to a general will expressed in a social contract between individuals and the state. Rousseau saw freedom and justice being achieved by the subordination of individual interests to a common good that is defined by equality rather than inequality. The debates between the natural law tradition and the communitarian tradition formed the background to the development of social thought in the 19th century. The possibilities for social harmony, social order, individual and collective freedom became increasingly focused around questions of equality and inequality as the industrial revolution gained momentum and its effects became increasingly obvious. Conventional political philosophies or ideologies, from liberalism on the right to Marxism on the left, are derived from such debates.

For Marxists, the concept and theory of ideology is central, though its meaning is different to that associated with conventional political philosophies/ideologies. Marx established how ideology originates and what its functions in society are. Being a historical materialist, he argued that it was not the consciousness of people that determines the course of history, but rather it is conflict over the productive process that shapes both the course of history and people's ideology (Marx, 1970). In capitalist societies, the ideas, values and beliefs of those who dominate the production, distribution and business sectors become accepted as the ideas of all sections of society, including those who stand to lose by their application in everyday affairs. One has only to witness the seeming triumph of neoliberalism/global capitalism, although perhaps the current 'credit crunch' and ensuing global recession will call this into question. Furthermore, the concept of ideology remains vital to the contemporary social sciences, despite those who argue that we have reached the end of ideology (Thompson, 1990)[6]. This is because when considering developments in relation to social work, the concept of ideology, and the use of theory more generally, is indispensable. It is impossible to understand the nature and function of welfare in general, and social work in particular, without an analysis of dominant social values and the social, economic and political systems in which they operate.

It is also important to note another aspect of Enlightenment and modernity, namely much of feminism. Initially, there was liberal feminism's preoccupation with equal rights for women and men, accompanied by a commitment to improve the position of women in society. The focus is on reform, with the state being seen as a neutral arbiter open to the influence of reason and political pressure (Wolf, 1993). On the other hand, Marxist/socialist feminism analyses the position of women in society within the context of a conventional Marxist analysis of capitalism with sexual oppression being a dimension of class power, but concludes that women's position cannot only be understood as a dimension of capitalism; rather, it is an element of patriarchical capitalism (see Beasley, 1999). Then again, radical feminism sees women as a group oppressed by men as a group, this having its roots in male and female biology (Bell and Klein, 1996).

Postmodernism

Turning to postmodernism, as well as often being seen as its forerunner, poststructuralism is often subsumed under it (Sarup, 1993). Both represent a rejection of the major tenets of Enlightenment and modernity, including Marxism and liberalism as well as scientific

—

13

modes of thought in which human history is claimed to represent a unilinear development (Lemert, 1994). Poststructuralism can be counterposed to structuralism, a collective label for a variety of loosely related philosophical traditions that emerged in France during the middle of the 20th century. They diverged in the source and identity of the underlying structures that shaped reality, but all subscribed to the idea that humans were made and operated by structures and forces beyond their personal and collective control (Gibbins, 1998).

Poststructuralism developed around a number of philosophers, most importantly Foucault (1977) whose work is an unremitting critique of Enlightenment epistemology. He argued that the latter prioritises the distinction between thinking and acting, whereas the history of Enlightenment theory and knowledge shows there are only ways of acting-thinking, or power-knowledge. Put another way, knowledge is normally regarded as providing us with the power to do things, a liberation, but Foucault inverts this, arguing that knowledge is a power over others, the power to define others thereby ceasing to be a liberation and becoming instead a mode of domination.

For Foucault, the notion of 'discourse' is important in seeing how social knowledges are organised and distributed, and how they affect social action. Societies have discourses about their social problems and social policies, with each discourse being structured or organised around central themes and connections, these defining the terms in which statements can be made, investigations can be conducted, and conversations can take place (Clarke and Cochrane, 1998). Such powers are not located in single institutions, but are undertaken by a range of social actors, particularly the 'psy professions' of social workers, psychologists, psychiatrists and criminologists. They are all involved in the exercising of 'disciplinary power' over others, and as these powers become more entrenched in the social order, so more and more people are drawn into the micro-technologies. No central authority, the argument continues, regulates or bestows them, but rather they are decentred and distributed throughout the social and institutional networks of the modern political order.

Poststructuralism is a challenge to conventional ways of interpreting the growth and development of social institutions of welfare including social work, with grand visions of progress and reform rejected in favour of more detailed assessments of the conditions of emergence, maintenance and contestation of specific welfare programmes. More broadly, it challenges the normative view of social science as the progressive accumulation of knowledge in the service of human value.

Postmodernism refers to an eclectic range of perspectives and beliefs about the contemporary world, as well as to the fundamental and complex transformations in the social, economic, cultural and technological spheres (Parton, 1996b). It is difficult not to accept the sense of the current pace of change and the need to draw attention to such things as the importance of difference and diversity, the significance and variety of new political strategies and movements, and the level of critique directed at a whole new range of previous assumptions, received wisdom and practices.

Smart (1993) points out that notions of postmodernism, postmodernity, postmodernisation and post-Fordism serve to describe the central features and processes of the various global transformations that have occurred recently, and which have also included a restructured welfare state (see, for example, Bourdieu, 1984; Bauman, 1991, 1992, 1997; Crook et al, 1992; Loader and Burrows, 1994; Lyon, 2000). But as important as these changes are, perhaps the most crucial elements in relation to the 'postmodern condition' are developments in the intellectual and epistemological spheres. Postmodernity sees us inhabiting a world that has become disoriented, disturbed and subject to doubt. Essential features of modernity, such as the pursuit of order, progress, science and rationality, are increasingly being undermined by a simultaneous range of negative conditions and experiences, together with the persistence of chance and threat of indeterminacy. Postmodernity, therefore, is characterised by the fragmentation of modernity into forms of institutional pluralism marked by variety, difference, contingency, relativism and ambivalence, all of which modernity sought to overcome. It is this constant and growing questioning of modern resolutions that has been diagnosed as symptomatic of the 'postmodern condition'.

Lyotard's *The Postmodern Condition* (1986) was the first to use the term 'postmodern' in relation to social science, defining it as 'incredulity towards meta narratives' (p xxiv). By this he meant that the advances of technology, the organisation of international capital and the ensuing changes in social and economic structures of modern societies had made all the old ideologies and theories redundant. In their place 'local narratives' come to dominate, these containing a diversity of values and beliefs held by a variety of groups that also involve shifting alliances in society with no agreed vision of the future. Lyotard, therefore, rejects totality, stressing instead the fragmentation of 'language games', of time, of the human subject and of society itself.

It is hard to disagree that there has been a loss of confidence in science, experts and politicians in terms of offering ways of solving economic, social and human problems. Increasingly, notions of ambivalence, contingency, risk and reflexivity are seen as characteristic of contemporary society, a society that has been be characterised as a risk society (Beck, 1992). Whereas in modern society communal concerns and values related to substantive and positive goals of social change, in the current risk society the normative basis is safety and the utopia is peculiarly negative and defensive – preventing the worst and protection from harm (Parton, 1996c).

Finally in relation to postmodernism, there is feminism to consider, particularly its 'paradigm shift' (Barrett and Philips, 1992) from finding the cause of women's oppression, part of the modern project, to celebrating women's difference from men (Williams, 1996). It was a move away from seeing oppression as rooted in social structure towards an emphasis on oppression as identity rooted in difference. This shift provided opportunities to explore the relationship between identity, subjectivity, subject position and political agency. Black feminism raised the issue of the need to acknowledge the ways in which existing social divisions reconstitute women's experiences of the world and that the category 'woman' is itself differentiated by, for example, class, 'race', ethnicity, disability, age and sexuality (for example, Hill-Collins, 1991). Going further, postmodern feminism involves a rejection of the idea of single explanations and opposition to essentialism, the belief that differences between men and women are innate rather than socially constructed (Gelsthorpe, 1997). There is also a celebration of a plurality of knowledges, and the so-called rationality and objectivity of contemporary science comes under attack, with attempts being made to create fluid, open terms and language that more clearly reflect women's experiences (for example, Benhabib, 1992).

Enlightenment, modernity and postmodernism revisited

The reader may be asking what that the discussion of Enlightenment and modernity together with postmodernism has to do with the development of social work. As examples, there are two issues I want to mention.

First, such concepts influence how developments in society are seen and understood. Put simply, for example, the zenith of social work, which resulted from the Seebohm Report (1968) and the subsequent creation of local authority social services departments, is clearly an Enlightenment project in line with modernity. These developments arose from the view that by utilising social science and reason, a new profession, social work, could be established, together with new organisations and structures for ways of delivering its services. All this would in turn help alleviate and ultimately solve social problems and society's ills as a whole. It corresponds to the social democratic consensus of the time: the belief that the state had a key role in dealing with social problems and difficulties. This can be counterposed to developments since those heady days, which have seen a breakdown of that consensus, the rise of the New Right and now the dominance of neoliberalism. And as far as social work is concerned, essentially my argument is that we have seen its deprofessionalisation. This has included the fragmentation of the social work task, the loss of social work autonomy and discretion, and increased bureaucracy and control involving the advance and now domination of managerialism. Ultimately, we have witnessed the demise of social services departments. Such developments can be seen in terms of the loss of faith in science and reason to find the cause of social problems and, in turn, in the ability of professionals, like social workers, to deal with and ultimately solve these problems. Instead, the best that can be done is to assess and manage the risk inherent in individuals' problems and difficulties. One can read this as the triumph of free market or neoliberal ideology, or alternatively as a move to the postmodern society.

—

Second, turning to practice, as we have seen social work can be regarded as an aspect of what Foucault (1977) termed 'disciplinary power' associated with the growth of the 'psy professions', together with the spread of new discourses and technologies of treatment and surveillance (Davis and Garrett, 2004). As a result, in understanding the dynamics of power relations, social workers have to interrogate the meaning of diversity, difference and division. Williams (1996, p 70), fusing feminism and postmodernism, does precisely this, arguing for social work to celebrate diversity, acknowledge difference and fight division. Diversity refers to 'difference claimed upon a shared collective [and specific] experience ... and not with a subordinated or unequal subject position', for example, shared language, nationality, 'race', age, sexual identity and so on. Difference refers to 'a situation where a shared collective experience/identity – say, around or combining gender, ethnicity, sexuality, religion, disability – forms the basis of resistance against the positioning of that identity as subordinate'. Finally, division means the 'translation of the expression of a shared experience into a form of domination', an example when being a white, British, heterosexual man 'forms an identity which protects a privileged position'. Furthermore, none of these categories is fixed or closed, so movement can take place from one to another. In brief, social workers should understand and embrace these issues in ways that work for rather than against service users as they strive for increased control and direction over their lives.

Enlightenment and modernity, together with postmodernism, are concepts that should be born in mind when reading this book. They are vital in any attempts to outline, analyse and understand the development of social work. But, going further, from which precise standpoint do I view all this?

The reader will surely have gathered that, despite the challenges of neoliberalism and postmodernism, I am a critical modernist in orientation, this being a critical stance relating to sociology, social theory, social policy and social work. Despite being marginalised in recent years, Marxism's coherence and logic in terms of providing a theory of society and theorisation of capitalism has not been surpassed, albeit it has to be complemented with aspects of 'race' and feminism. It covers pre-history and history and extends to the present, also providing, or at least sketching, a future. It involves a materialist interpretation of history and a view that economic life is central, if not actually causative or determining, over most collective aspects of life in society and over many of the individual aspects of life from which a collectivity arises. Marx was even able to paint a picture of what is now called 'globalisation'. As Hobsbawm (1998, cited in Callinicos, 1999) points out, what might in 1848 have struck an uncommitted reader as revolutionary rhetoric – or at best a plausible prediction – can now be read as a concise characteristic of capitalism at the end of the 20th and now in the 21st century. Current events in relation to the global economic crisis surely confirm such a view. Even Giddens, by no means a Marxist, stresses that 'capitalist markets still have many of the damaging consequences to which Marx pointed, including the dominance of the growth ethic, universal commodification and economic polarisation…. The critiques of these tendencies surely remain as important as ever was' (1994, pp 11-12).

Meanwhile, postmodernism is an intellectual current that bruised the self-confidence to which notions such as reason, science and knowledge had become accustomed, although it can be subjected to many criticisms. First, and most obviously, although postmodernism, and particularly Lyotard, is incredulous about grand or meta-narratives, it is itself one because it argues that all meta-narratives and ideologies are redundant. Second, at the heart of postmodernism is a radical individualism that rejects class, 'race', gender, indeed all bases of collective identity, since they are all premised on a wider narrative about how the world works (Ferguson, 2008). From this, postmodernism sits too well with governments that prioritise individual expenditure over public welfare. Third, and consistent with the emphasis on individualism, is the postmodern rejection of structural explanations of poverty. Finally, there is postmodernism's moral relativism, which refuses to privilege any discourse over another, thereby leading to the charge of nihilism.

It can also be said that many postmodern insights have now simply become part and parcel of the disciplines it once challenged (for example, Leonard, 1997). As such, critical realism (Lopez and Potter, 2001) offers a more reasonable and useful framework from which to engage with current philosophical, scientific and social scientific challenges. Although it developed from a critique of positivism in natural science, it puts forward epistemological caution with respect to scientific knowledge, as opposed to self-defeating relativist scepticism. Knowledge is culturally and historically situated and progress in terms of accumulation of knowledge is not simply a historically linear phenomenon. Regression is, therefore, possible, but it is important to emphasise that so too is progress, and human knowledge has indeed expanded over the centuries. This is not the place to expound on critical realism further, suffice to say that there is close affinity with the critical theory of the Frankfurt School and its second-generation representative Habermas. Similarly, it has an affinity with Marxism in that those involved in seeking to understand the world are precisely those who seek to change it, this being the ultimate goal of radical/critical social work.

The book: structure and organisation

As the title indicates, this book looks at the rise and subsequent fall of social work as a profession. It does not aim to be comprehensive or to provide an all-embracing examination of social work's development. Bearing in mind my experience of social work, I focus on policy and practice developments in relation to children and families, including young offenders, while also commenting on other user areas.

Echoing the 'locating myself' section above, and like Garrett (2003), what follows is not an objective or 'true' account of the rise and fall of social work. Rather, the aim is more limited, this being to unsettle or question dominant and official accounts of what has occurred, while at the same time wanting to avoid a somewhat quirky polemic. It is an invitation for readers to question and rethink what has occurred. Although I accept that social work is an arena of struggle and contestation, the future it has does, or at least should, borrow from the past.

Social work has been around for a long time but as an occupation certainly reached a high point in the 1970s when it was the rising star of the human service professions. In Woodroofe's (1962) terms, this essentially involved the move from charity to social work. Since then, coinciding with changed ideological, political and economic circumstances, it has been under attack from the media and politicians. Practitioners' expertise and effectiveness have been questioned and they are blamed for scandals, notably in relation to abused children and most recently in relation to Baby Peter[7]. There have also been continuing changes in their organisation and day-to-day practice, which, despite arguments about professionalisation, actually amounts to deprofessionalisation. The result is that instead of a profession based on knowledge, understanding, skills and collegial relations, we now have a so-called profession whereby managers dominate, their focus being on budgetary controls, targets and form and computer exemplar completion. Little face-to-face work occurs with users, as a relationship-based profession has been transformed into a bureaucratic one focusing on the assessment and rationing of resources and services. Furthermore, it has been forced into a more controlling, moral-policing role, with users often told to change their lives or face the consequences, which could include losing their children or their liberty. We have also seen the demise of the Central Council for Education and Training in Social Work (CCETSW) and the National Institute of Social Work (NISW). Social work itself is rarely mentioned in government circles except negatively when things go wrong in relation to child abuse tragedies. My central argument, therefore, is that at best what remains of social work is a limited version of what the possibilities once were. It seems timely, therefore, to have a critical look at the profession's rise and arguably subsequent fall.

Chapter Two looks at the beginnings of social work to its 1970s peak. Its roots lie in the socioeconomic changes of the 18th and 19th centuries, but various pioneers were influential in the early development, including the Charity Organisation Society (Younghusband, 1981). The first half of the 20th century saw advances in terms of social legislation such as housing and secondary education. However, apart from such as the establishment of the mental health social work course at the London School of Economics in the late 1920s, developments in social work slowed down. It was during the 1940s that things picked up and the value of trained social work staff became more accepted, these including almoners in hospitals, psychiatric social workers, and childcare and family caseworkers.

—

Importantly, the welfare state was established and the social democratic consensus took hold. Welfare services were established for the elderly and people with special needs, as well as unified services for children, with both being provided by local authorities. Following the Seebohm Report (1968), these welfare and children's services were amalgamated into local authority social services departments. By this time, NISW was doing much to advance social work, and in 1970 BASW was formed. Psychology and sociology provided a knowledge base, with psychoanalysis dominating prior to many other theory-practice developments. Group and community work, in addition to casework, also featured. Professional training also changed significantly, with the certificate of qualification in social work being established in 1971 by CCETSW. In short, the foregoing indicates the increasing influence and professionalisation of social work, such developments being congruent with the Enlightenment project.

The election of Margaret Thatcher as prime minister in 1979 ushered in profound changes in the ideological, political and economic spheres, all of which were to negatively affect social work. Her premiership and that of John Major, together with their impact on social work, are the concerns of Chapter Three[8]. The New Right employed classical liberal critiques of state action, applying them to contemporary issues of economic and social policy, including preferring market to public sector approaches to welfare. Social workers were to feel the brunt of this changed political and economic climate. For example, in the late 1980s and 1990s, the introduction of managerialism from the private sector led to the beginnings of the deprofessionalisation of social work, especially in relation to older people, by the introduction of care management. As for methods, perhaps surprisingly, it was still possible to utilise community and group work as well as casework because of the influence of the Barclay Report (1982), which advocated community social work. Later, the Diploma in Social Work was introduced and advances continued in relation to knowledge/theory, for example, witness developments into anti-racist/discriminatory/oppressive practice during the 1980s and 1990s. Overall, however, the Thatcherite period witnessed the triumph of neoliberalism and/or the challenges from postmodernism.

—

Arguably, we see the beginnings of the move from social work back to charity, at least in terms of service provision.

Social work's decline accelerated during the New Labour years after the election of Tony Blair in 1997 and during Gordon Brown's time as prime minister. These are the concerns of Chapter Four. Despite talk of the 'Third Way', New Labour has largely continued with Thatcherism or neoliberalism, including a sustained ideological and material investment in the superiority of 'market society'. One consequence has been the increased privatisation of services, as well the use of the voluntary sector in the provision of services. Social work is now often subsumed under 'social care'; it is no longer a qualification for probation, nor does it have the central role it had in relation to young offending, and the approved social worker role in relation to mental health has also been diluted. The General Social Care Council has replaced CCETSW and there has been the demise of social services departments. Similarly, we have seen the end of NISW, and although a new social work degree and various post-qualifying courses have been introduced, social work itself is ever more dominated by managerialism. What remains is essentially limited to rationing and risk assessment, which has to be carried out as speedily as possible under the direction of managers. In the process, opportunities for community and group work are severely curtailed. To the extent that preventative social work does take place, it usually involves other 'professionals' as neoliberalism and/or postmodernism continues to hold sway.

Chapter Five charts the changes in the professional education and training of social workers over the past 40 years, culminating in the introduction of the social work degree and post-qualification awards under New Labour. Arguments often centre on the increased professionalisaton required in today's complex, (post)modern world. However, employer involvement in training and the introduction of competences models have challenged social work's professional autonomy and prepare social workers for working in more regulated and regulating ways. Some argue that this provides more opportunities as social work adapts to a more diverse welfare system that has less professional dominance and more accountability in both welfare and education systems (Cannan, 1994/95). My response is that

—

at best this is an optimistic view, with one only having to look at developments following New Labour's 'modernisation' agenda. There is less emphasis on the academic knowledge and understanding required to practice social work, and more emphasis on competences. The result is that social work has actually been deprofessionalised, the task has been fragmented further, and there is a preoccupation with form/computer exemplar filling so as to meet the targets and performance indicators instigated by managers at the behest of New Labour. Again reiterating earlier comments, what remains of social work is a limited version of what it used to be.

Chapter Six takes a critical look at two other key themes over recent times, namely the growth of managerialism and the development of the 'social work business' (Harris, 2003). Since the 1980s, more effective private sector-type management has been presented as the panacea for almost every problem facing the public services, including social work. It was hoped such managers would overthrow the bureaucratic and professional barriers to change, thereby creating a vibrant mixed economy of care. Consequently, the introduction of managerialism and the social work business have taken social work away from relationship-based activity, let alone anything more radical, critical or even progressive. The rhetoric refers to 'empowerment', 'choice' and 'needs-led assessment', and there is an attempt to recreate the 'client' or 'service user' as a 'consumer'/'customer', particularly as in the personalisation agenda. However, the counter argument is that social work is now operating in a quasi-business regime that subordinates the public's needs and the skills of social workers to the demands of competition within the social care market. Significantly, we often see social care organisations having to adapt to meet their targets rather than the real needs of the people they are supposed to serve.

Despite this, there are many who manage to retain a sense of optimism for the future of social work (for example, Garrett, 2003, 2009b; Jordan, 2007, 2008, 2010; Ferguson, 2008; Ferguson and Woodward, 2009). The conclusion of the book involves a discussion of such views, views that continue to see social work as being compatible with values of social justice and of seeking social change, despite the current dominant belief that neoliberalism is here to stay and is the best we can hope for. This latter comment is particularly apt, given the election of a Conservative–Liberal Democrat coalition government in May 2010. Even so, these optimistic perspectives cannot be easily dismissed, but in some ways I also act as the devil's advocate. I put forward the argument that although people are likely to be always engaged in activities that were the preserve of professional social work, or could be called social work, such activities are increasingly being carried out by an array of advisers, mentors and care/support/ project workers. Importantly, these 'professionals' are less qualified than social workers, cheaper to employ and easier to control. This rather depressing scenario is not set in stone, but, at best, perhaps future social work will indeed be a far limited version of what it once was and what it could have achieved, while at worst, it will no longer exist as a single professional occupation.

Finally, in pursuing my argument, I do not want to be too oriented to the past, to the 'golden age' of social work of the 1970s. No profession or set of working practices can remain fixed in uncertain and changing times, but what I want to emphasise is that the changes that have occurred have taken place within the framework of neoliberalism. As we will see, to the extent that there may have been progressive aspects in the 'modernising' agenda, they have been constrained or nullified in the individualistic world in which we currently live.

Notes

[1] Throughout the book, I tend to use the term 'service user' or 'user' rather than the previously used 'client' because it implies a more equal relationship between social workers and the people they work with. Although New Labour wanted such people to be referred to as 'consumers' or 'customers', this is a contested term, not least as far as social workers and users themselves are concerned.

[2] ICS is supposed to provide a framework, method of practice and a *business* process to support practitioners and managers in undertaking assessment, planning, intervention and review. However, there are many flaws with the system, as is discussed in Chapter Four.

[3] The Common Assessment Framework was introduced by the Department for Children, Schools and Families in 2006, the aim being to introduce a standardised approach (using forms/computer exemplars) for all professionals working in

children's services to assess a child's additional needs and decide how they should be met. Again, this is discussed more fully in Chapter Four.

[4] Intermediate treatment was introduced by the 1969 Children's and Young Persons Act as a supplement to ordinary supervision orders for young offenders. It was hoped that the development of specialist services for such young people – for instance, case/group work, leisure/recreational pursuits, education – would lead to less delinquency and less need for custody.

[5] 'Race' is a socially constructed concept rather than a biological category because there are no inherent biological characteristics or traits attributable to racial origins, hence the use of inverted comas here and throughout this book.

[6] The 'end of ideology' thesis first made an appearance in the 1960s. For example, Bell (1960) and Lipset (1963) argued that as capitalist industrialisation and welfare provision had secured affluence for all, ideological debates between capitalism and socialism were redundant. Then again, Fukuyama (1992) argued that logic, historical evidence and (the then) recent events in Eastern Europe showed that democracy and capitalism had triumphed over all other systems and there was no alternative to them. There are also elements of 'end of ideology' in postmodernism; for example, Lyotard's (1986) argument that grand ideologies can no longer provide valid explanations for social, economic and political processes or act as guides to future utopia. However, the idea that we somehow live in a post-ideological age is successfully challenged by Schwarzmantel (2008).

[7] Baby Peter was a 17-month-old boy who died in August 2007 from severe injuries inflicted while in the care of his mother, her partner and a lodger in the household. In November 2008, the two men were found guilty of causing or allowing the death of a child. The mother had already pleaded guilty to the same charge. Baby Peter had also been the subject of a child protection plan following concerns he was being abused or neglected. After the convictions, the death of Baby Peter and the inadequate responses of child welfare professionals dominated political and media discourses and resulted in the setting up of a Social Work TaskForce to examine the recruitment, training and overall quality and status of social work in England. It reported in November 2009 (SWTF, 2009) and is discussed further in Chapters Five and Seven.

[8] For convenience, from here onwards I refer to the Thatcher/Major years as 'Thatcherism'. Margaret Thatcher was prime minister for the majority of the period in question (1979-90) and her policies, together with the underlying ideological/ political philosophy of neoliberalism, were continued by John Major (1990-97).

TWO

The beginnings of social work to its 1970s zenith

Rather unhelpfully, the *Concise Oxford English Dictionary* does not define 'social work' and merely defines a 'social worker' as a 'person trained for social service'. 'Social service' is then simply stated to be 'philanthropic activity'. Actually, what amounts to social work, helping people with problems and difficulties or in need, has always existed; it was carried out by family, friends, neighbours and volunteers (McLaughlin, 2008). What differentiates social work as a distinct activity is that it can be seen as *organised helping* originating in organisational responses to social changes arising from socioeconomic developments in the 19th century (Payne, 2005a). It can be viewed as an extension of our natural humanity as we are by nature social, empathetic and thus altruistic, this equating with a Marxist view of human nature. Conversely, social work can be understood as being needed to stifle the baser instincts of individuals who, being selfish and greedy, are less likely to help their fellows, especially at times of conflict or when there are scarce resources. Again, it is possible to link this to a Marxist understanding of current society as dominated by the greed and selfishness inherent in global capitalism.

The Protestant Reformation, the Renaissance and the Enlightenment were influential in the development of social welfare in Britain. They helped reduce the role and power of the churches, while municipal and charitable provision simultaneously increased, with charitable provision being greatly influenced by Judeo-Christian ideas and facilitated by the emergence of a middle class willing to take on local responsibility. Charitable and municipal provision was increasingly interconnected with arrangements emanating from central government. In 1601, the Poor Law placed the responsibility for the care of those in dire need on local parishes, and the 1662 Act of Settlement enabled the parish overseer to remove from the parish

—

any settler who could not show they could find work within 40 days (McLaughlin, 2008). Then, as the industrial revolution progressed, central government became increasingly involved in welfare, often as a result of having to maintain order. With people increasingly moving away from their rural tight-knit communities to the towns and cities, there was increasing concern about moral breakdown, crime and health. The health of the poor became a particular concern for the ruling and intellectual classes because of concerns relating to military expansion abroad and the resulting need for a healthy military force. While many saw the masses as lacking proper morals or values as a result of deficient guidance or poor breeding, others saw that capitalism was creating inequalities and social problems and that ameliorating measures were necessary. At the same time, the Chartists were demanding the vote for working men, while trade unionism was on the rise, with political developments around issues of class becoming significant (Powell, 2001). Fear of the masses then, as well as an element of altruism and self-interest, were all factors in the early stages of the development of welfare and social work.

In examining the development of social work, this chapter begins by looking at the prevailing political, economic, social and ideological situation that was initially dominated by liberalism. Thereafter, it deals with social work's early pioneers before a discussion of events during the first half of the 20th century, which amounted to a relative stalling of developments in social work, although this was less the case in the welfare field more generally (Younghusband, 1981). The chapter then goes on to cover the comparative frantic activity of the postwar years until social work's high point of the 1970s, which coincided with the social democratic consensus of the time.

Liberalism and the early pioneers

In his *Second Treatise of Government* published in 1690, Locke provides the essentials of liberalism, the political doctrine that holds that the purpose of the state, as an association of independent individuals, is to facilitate the happiness of its members. Today it is possible to talk of *liberalisms*, with some versions being extremely individualistic and others more open to collective strategies for social and political development (Gray, 1989). Given this caveat, the fundamental values of liberalism are the overlapping principles of liberty and freedom, together with individualism. Liberty and freedom are seen in negative terms as the absence of coercion, while individualism emphasises the ability of individuals to pursue their own self-interest free from state intervention, which will, by means of Adam Smith's invisible hand, lead to the well-being of all. Another value is inequality, in that liberty and freedom are incompatible with equality on the assumption that the rich will not share their wealth voluntarily so substantial government intervention would be required. In the last analysis, it is not possible for liberals to be both for and against government or state intervention, with arguments against such intervention centring on it being socially disruptive and wasteful of resources and obliterating individual freedom (George and Wilding, 1976).

The bedrock for liberalism, Adam Smith's *Wealth of Nations*, appeared in 1776, arguing for market forces operating *freely* under competition. *Free* trade and *free* markets formed the liberal or classical school of economics. It amounted to a strong belief in the rational, self-correcting market. All this did not sit easily with the state intervention of the Poor Law, despite the fact that the relief it offered was minimal. Other important and influential figures were Malthus, Ricardo and, in a different vein, Bentham (Fraser, 1973) and Darwin.

Malthus' *Essay on the Principle of Population* was published in 1798 and argued that unless restrained, population growth would outstrip the means of subsistence, leading to misery for the masses and ultimately war involving everyone. This was especially so because poor relief encouraged improvident marriages and inducements to population growth. Ricardo's *Principles of Political Economy* appeared in 1817 and introduced the 'iron law of wages'. Its central argument was that as only a certain proportion of the national wealth was available as wages, the more paid out in poor relief, the less remained for wages. Both Malthus and Ricardo saw the Poor Law as counterproductive, self-defeating and a cause of the problems it was trying to combat, and these views were very influential at the time.

Jeremy Bentham also accepted the free market, but realised that at times the state might have to intervene, although he emphasised that any intervention had to be geared to the needs of individualism. He

—

accepted Samuel Smiles' espousal of self-help as being the supreme virtue and of being the ideal way forward, but he devised a test of utility for those occasions when the state really had to get involved. This was applied to institutions: were they efficient and economical and, above all, did they provide the 'greatest happiness of the greatest number'? The Benthamites or utilitarians were a source of many of the reforms of the 19th century, which included elementary education and some basic medical services.

Also important to liberalism was Charles Darwin's *The Origin of Species*, published in 1859, which was subsequently applied to the social sphere. This interpretation counteracted much of the extreme pessimism of Malthus, with Spencer (1940 [1884]) arguing that the welfare of everyone would be best served by allowing the weak and underdeveloped sections of society to die out, leaving behind the fittest to transmit the highest achievements and powers to the next generation.

The pioneers

Although socioeconomic factors are at the root of the growth of social work, by the middle of the 19th century three pioneers could be identified (Younghusband, 1981). These were the Charity Organisation Society (COS), one of its leaders Octavia Hill, and Canon Barnett and his wife at Toynbee Hall Settlement. They had a Christian view of the value of people to each other and the sort of society they should promote. This included traditional values of individual and family life, which were imbued with the prevailing liberal ideals, although they were also concerned with new forms of friendship between members of different classes. The COS was founded in 1869 as the Society for the Organisation of Charitable Relief and Repressing Mendicity and it extolled the moral virtues of self-help and necessary personal sacrifice on the part of the poor. Octavia Hill was involved in social housing and made a practical contribution to material difficulties as well as being involved in the moral regeneration of the inhabitants of city slums. The Barnetts founded the settlement movement in 1884, with more settlements following both within and outside the capital. All three pioneering groups were part of a philanthropic movement that was a counterpart to the rational individualism embedded in liberal political theory. Although often less acknowledged, there was an emphasis on the 'moral economy' of social relationships rather than just the material economy of capitalist industrialised development. This reflected a view of the true value of society lying in the bonds between individual members, of the value of the social over the individual, and of people working together for the common good (Jordan, 2007).

The importance of women in these early days of social work has to be acknowledged. Social relations for men arose mainly from their work but for women they arose mainly from their domestic role, so when women worked outside the domestic sphere it tended to be in caring, social welfare roles (McLaughlin, 2008). In any case, the pioneers were all shocked and concerned about the mass poverty and overcrowding, brutality and ignorance that confronted them. According to Younghusband (1981), the doyenne of British social work for much of the last century, the resulting charitable work made advances in relation to five areas, namely knowledge, usable knowledge, methods, training, and organisational structure and procedure. Admittedly, the areas referred to might seem a little idiosyncratic today, but they do give a flavour of the concerns of a developing profession and as such it is worth commenting on them a little further.

First, knowledge was bound up in the prevailing political ideology of liberalism, which included the deterrent Poor Law based on the 'iron law of wages', the Malthusian theory of population, Benthamism and, later, Darwinism applied to society. Marxist theories had little influence at the time, while subjects such as sociology and psychology were still emerging, so generally social science knowledge was limited. Instead, there were centuries-old ideas about the absolute rights of the father over his children and, to a large extent, his wife. There was unquestioned belief in the Protestant work ethic and the pioneers had a strong Christian motivation expressed in the belief in the equality of people, although the class system was not questioned. They were clearer about obligations than rights, with their ideal society being one that recognised mutual obligations between rich and poor.

—

Second, usable knowledge was based on direct experience and was likely to be expressed in moral terms. However, the pioneers began to keep records and discuss their experiences, trying to draw deductions and conclusions in the process. They wanted to discover more about what made people behave in certain ways rather than simply relying on individual, narrowly prejudiced experience. Even so, the religious urge and prevailing individualist philosophy led to a focus on the individual, on what they called 'character', to be supported if it were there or deplored if it were not. As a result, poverty and drunkenness, for example, were primarily seen as due to lack of thrift, a failure of moral will, rather than to the constraints of economic or social conditions.

Third, there was a need to work out and discover social work methods, with the COS being the originator of casework, that is, the process of individualising people through enquiry. This included trying to ascertain all the relevant factors involved in the presenting situation, making a plan with the 'applicant', giving help adequate to meet need (if, indeed, help was given) and following the case through. The system was mainly concerned with extreme material need, preventing pauperism and encouraging thrift. People were categorised as either 'deserving' or 'undeserving', admittedly an oversimplified and moralistic division that was later changed to the little better 'helpable' and 'unhelpable'. The 'helpable' were those who could overcome a crisis or series of crises with support. The 'unhelpable' formed two groups: those who were too demoralised, shiftless or malevolent to respond and could only be left to the Poor Law; and those whose needs were so long term because of illness, old age and the like, that they were beyond the resources of a voluntary society. The focus was on the *circumstances* of each individual rather than on the individual as such, indicating 'that it was possible for a well regulated authority to manage and administer social problems without undermining ideals of individual responsibility for poverty and personal responsibility for collective assistance' (O'Brien and Penna, 1998 p 26). It promised a form of social administration that supported the principles of economic individualism.

The COS, like Octavia Hill and the Barnetts, emphasised treating people as individuals and as equals. Friendship, or at any rate some sort of relationship other than the more patronising and arrogant style of earlier good works, was recognised as being necessary. It may be difficult to understand what equality and friendship meant when there was so much inequality around, but perhaps paternalism could occasionally be transcended by the mutual recognition that we are all human. This was all to become the concept of making and using a relationship in the interest of the client, together with treating them with dignity. It is a sad comment on social work today that the pioneers' emphasis on the value of relationships needs restating, re-emphasising and re-recognising today.

In her work with tenants and the settlement movement led by the Barnetts, Octavia Hill discovered the value of group discussions, activities and outings. What was later to be called community organisation, community work or even a community orientation for the caseworker was also important in her work. She initiated bulk buying for resale to tenants, trade training schemes and many forms of recreation, and campaigned for open spaces. The COS actually thought that 'organising the district', meaning coordinating local charities on COS principles, was more important than casework. Meanwhile, the Barnetts initiated the Stepney Council on Public Welfare, whose objects included not only charity but also 'all matters affecting the welfare of the district' (Barnett, 1918, p 633, cited in Younghusband, 1981, p 13). Despite the work of Hill and the COS, it is the Barnetts who are generally seen as the originators of community work.

Fourth, when it came to social work training, Octavia Hill had to train her co-workers, while the COS trained volunteers for the actual work with 'applicants' and Canon Barnett conducted searching group discussions with settlement residents about individual motivation. Eventually, some of these people were to be called social workers. Such training remained a kind of apprenticeship preparation in a work setting, with the first real beginning of education for social work occurring in 1895. The Women's University Settlement set up a joint lectures committee between the settlement itself, the COS and the National Union of Women Workers. The lectures related to practical experience and covered the Poor Law, charity and almsgiving. Later a paid lecturer was appointed, the course lengthened and lectures added on 'the family and character', 'thoroughness' and 'personal work'. A whole term was also devoted to provisions for children, and in 1898 a COS special committee on training said it would like to see in the society the nucleus of a future university devoted to social science for those who planned to undertake philanthropic work (Smith, 1965, cited in Younghusband, 1981).

Finally, in considering the organisational structure and procedures through which help could be most effectively provided, the COS had a central office that coordinated the work of over 40 district committees all over London. The local offices were easily accessible to applicants and other agencies, while the workers could get to know and be known in the district. The COS central office also conducted enquiries, ran conferences and produced publications. Much of this resonates with the community social work aspirations of the 1980s and, in my view, continues to have relevance today.

Although the COS, Octavia Hill and the Barnetts were the key pioneers in the development of social work, this is not to say others did not play significant parts. The Salvation Army and the police court missioners of the Church of England Temperance Society tried to help the 'unhelpable'. The missioners' work in the courts included the supervision of offenders and matrimonial conciliation, and they were to emerge later as probation officers. Child welfare and protection were the remit of the National Society for the Prevention of Cruelty to Children, the National Children's Home and Dr Barnado's, all being established from the 1880s onwards. Dr Barnado started workshops for unemployed boys as well as turning a gin palace into a coffee palace, which was much like a modern-day community centre. He also diversified his provision for children as experience was gained and he became more practised in money raising. There were, for instance, homes for babies and toddlers, grouped cottage homes with a matron in charge of about 25 girls or boys of all ages, hospital schools for severely disabled children, a naval training school, a school of printing, and a system of boarding out in country foster homes.

All these activities signified the beginnings of social work, setting it on the convoluted road to becoming a profession. Although it did not involve a lengthy period of training like the medical or legal professions, and was never to gain as much autonomy as those professions, a code of ethics, a distinctive and recognised training, a body of literature and a professional association were all to emerge. These early years also anticipated much of what was to become social work a hundred or so years later, despite, as we will see, subsequent setbacks. These developments include casework and group and community work methods, records and procedures, formal training and even social services departments with central headquarters and outlying local/district offices. It is also possible to discern the beginnings of evidence-based practice. However, at the end of the 19th century, there was a clash of social and political attitudes and resultant conflict between COS leaders such as Charles Loch, Helen Bosanquet and Octavia Hill, and two of the leading Fabians, Sydney and Beatrice Webb. This confrontation postponed the reform of the Poor Law and arguably delayed the implementation of the welfare state.

The COS believed in the deterrent Poor Law, thinking that by thrift and prudence, together with help from relatives, friends and neighbours, the poor could live independent lives and save for ill health and old age. They opposed state provision in the form of, for example, old age pensions or school meals because they believed it would pauperise people and undermine incentives for work. On the other hand, the Webbs pointed to the inefficiency of the Poor Law, as it could not take action to prevent destitution or properly set people up again. They argued that faced with the degrading poverty in the slums of the towns and cities arising from the industrial revolution and the resulting disease, ill health and early death, it was not surprising that people aged prematurely or turned to drink and that thrift was not a practical priority. The Webbs argued that moral failure lay with the employers of exploited labourers, slum landlords and the ignorant and greedy rich. They saw the remedy in collective action against collective ills, such as extending and enforcing housing, health and conditions of work legislation. All this was reinforced by Charles Booth's enquiry into the life and labour of the people of London, which started to appear in 1883. Engels' (2005 [1887]) important work, *The Condition of the Working Class in England*, also became available in English. By now the philanthropic and individualist, moral view of poverty was being eroded as Fabianism began to make inroads.

Fabianism and the first half of the 20th century

Marx and Engels (1996) originally published their communist manifesto in 1848 and this, together with Marx's substantial body of work, was having a considerable influence on developments in Europe during the 1900s (O'Brien and Penna, 1998). Marx analysed the dynamics of capitalist production and development, focusing on capitalism resulting in a structural inequality of power between a dominant class and a subordinate class who are reduced to the status of commodities by having to sell their labour power in the market. A major thrust is a critique of liberalism, particularly the view that social reproduction is carried out by numerous atomised individuals engaging in free and equal market exchanges. The notion of 'individualism' is viewed as a mystification of the social character of production because humans never produce simply as individuals but as members of a definite form of society. Producing also involves relationships with other people that are structured by the economic organisation of society, and in capitalist societies individuals are not at all free and equal as these societies are based on class domination and exploitation. Such views were to be influential until well into the 1970s.

The Fabian Society, led by George Bernard Shaw, had much in common with Marxism, although its advocates differed in believing that capitalism could be transformed peacefully. Fabian socialists had three central values: equality, freedom and fellowship (George and Wilding, 1976). Equality, the argument went, led to social unity, efficiency, justice and individual self-realisation. For example, cooperation was needed to resolve the country's economic ills, but this simply could not happen if there was a continuing class struggle that had its roots in social and economic inequalities. It meant much more than equality of opportunity and should not be seen merely in negative terms – freedom from restraint – but as something positive, being preceded and accompanied by equalising measures. Freedom involves a concern for equality because inequality results in some

—

being in bondage to others. It also extends from the political into the economic sphere, a voice in conditions of work, and involves government action rather than inaction. Fellowship refers to cooperation rather than competition, an emphasis on the good of the community rather than the wants of individuals, on altruism rather than self-help, and on duties rather than rights. Some Fabians saw the role of government as being the eradication of capitalism by the widespread extension of public ownership, while others argued that capitalism could be tamed and harnessed to socialist aims, with the mixed economy becoming the end of the journey rather than the staging post. Either way, there was a belief in purposeful government action, the task being to regulate, even supplant, the market system in the interests of equality, freedom and fellowship. Fabians believed that through gradualism and permeation the capitalist state could be persuaded to reform itself with, in due course, the welfare state being evidence of this.

In fact, the beginnings of the welfare state lay with the Liberal prime minister Lloyd George and the introduction of provisions such as school meals in 1906, old age pensions in 1908 and national insurance to fund sickness, unemployed and widows benefits in 1911 (see Fraser, 1973). Some of the factors leading to these developments have already been mentioned: the fear of disorder and the need for a healthy military, together with elements of altruism and self-interest more generally. Another key consideration was the growing power and influence of social democracy in much of continental Europe at the beginning of the 20th century, which was later to influence the Labour Party, particularly its Fabian wing. Following Lloyd George's tenure, the interwar years were dominated by the depression years of the 1930s, which resulted in further welfare developments. These included the expansion of state education, a focus on housing, improvements to the Poor Law, and the provision of public health measures and even an embryonic municipal hospital service. Unemployment benefits were also extended and public works schemes introduced to cope with unemployment. These advances evolved pragmatically, were uncoordinated and were not universal, but, when compared with what happened to social work over the same period, they were important and substantial.

—

The stalling of social work

So what did actually occur in terms of social work? One of the original pioneers, Octavia Hill, sat on the 1905-09 Royal Commission on the Poor Laws and signed the majority report that recommended retaining an improved Poor Law. Beatrice Webb, meanwhile, signed the minority report recommending its abolition and replacement with specialised services for unemployment, health and education. Younghusband (1981) argued that the abolition of the Poor Law was undoubtedly right and that the majority missed the chance to recommend a new type of personal social services that could be slipped into the old structure and bring forward by 60 years what was eventually to become the Seebohm reorganisation.

Meanwhile, Toynbee Hall continued to produce social research, including Beveridge's study of unemployment, which shifted the unemployment problem from the individual worker to wider societal factors. Additionally, the Webbs continued their studies of various neglected social ills such as factory conditions, housing, education, the condition of the poor and colonialism.

Despite the advances in welfare provision, for much of the next 40 years 'initiative and fresh discovery died down in social work' (Younghusband, 1981, p 45). While the large-scale public services were being established, social workers were conspicuous by their absence. Exceptions included hospital almoners in voluntary and a few municipal hospitals, untrained police court missioners and social workers working in child guidance clinics. The 1907 Probation of Offenders Act and the 1925 Criminal Justice Act at first permitted and then required the appointment of probation officers to be paid from public funds to 'advise, assist and befriend' offenders. The first child guidance clinic opened in 1927 largely to help schools deal with unruly pupils. Most social workers, whether trained or untrained, were employed as moral welfare workers in voluntary family welfare agencies, mainly giving financial help, in the Invalid Children's Aid Association. The continued emphasis on relief giving and morality was clearly apparent. Furthermore, if we return to the five areas of progress mentioned earlier – knowledge, usable knowledge, method, training, organisational structure and procedures – despite some exceptions, we can clearly see a loss of momentum.

Knowledge derived from research rather than broad theory advanced unevenly; while social surveys and studies of poverty extended earlier work, broader sociological and psychological research studies were lacking. Freud's ideas regarding the individual psyche, with the unconscious explaining individual problems, took time to take hold in social work in Britain. Usable knowledge did not advance much either, with social workers learning from little but their own experience and the policy of the agency. Even the practice wisdom thereby gained was not properly recorded, organised, evaluated and disseminated. Method also languished, with the close relationship between case, group and community work being broken, so that only casework was seen as distinctively social work. An exception was a breakthrough regarding method in the US when Richmond (1917) developed her view of social diagnosis whereby information was gathered about the person concerned, the problem diagnosed, the solution identified and a treatment plan made.

Training fared a little better as advances were made in the early 1900s. The COS established the School of Sociology in London in 1903, which was later incorporated into the London School of Economics (LSE). In 1904, the Liverpool School of Social Science was jointly started by the University of Liverpool, a local settlement and the Liverpool COS. The London course included both theory and practice. Theory included elements of social theory and philosophy, economics, and social and economic history, but by the 1920s there was only a tenuous link between all this and practice. This was because the COS was frozen in an outmoded pattern of practical experience that had little educational content, while universities refrained from vocational training. More positively, in 1929 the first mental health course was established at the LSE and this did combine theory and practice. Then in 1936 the first publicly funded training board was set up by the Home Office, providing fees and grants for probation students to undertake social science and probation training.

Finally, limited progress was made in terms of organisational structure and procedures. For example, almoners, probation officers and some psychiatric social workers were employed in agencies whose

—

primary purpose and professional expertise were not social work. Social workers therefore had to discover how to make an effective contribution in interdisciplinary situations, something that retains its relevance today following the demise of social services departments. One important innovation, however, was the establishment by the Home Office of inspectorates for probation services as well as approved schools and some children's homes. Such inspectorates were to eventually become standard-setting, information-sharing, advisory and consultative services. These can be contrasted with the inspection and regulatory organisations of today, which have become obsessed with targets and performance indicators, and which are discussed in more detail later.

Social work and renewed activity

Social work's evolution may have slowed down in the early part of the 20th century, but there was some renewed activity during the 1940s. As the Second World War unfolded, a close association developed between warfare and welfare, so much so that personal social services ceased being considered as a form of poor relief. A major factor was the mass evacuation from many towns and cities of school children, mothers and younger children, as well as those made homeless by air raids. Local authorities were unable to cope with the range and extent of evacuation problems, not just in terms of the lack of required equipment but also in terms of the social and human costs arising from the loss, confusion and uncertainty associated with evacuation. These included misunderstandings between the evacuees and their new hosts, particularly teenage boys. Titmuss (1950) went so far as to point out that the social dimension of the situation and the resultant support needed began to be identified simply by its manifest absence. The problem became so bad that in 1940, in order to prevent protests from angry householders in reception areas, hostels had to be established for 'difficult' children whose problems included incontinence, running away, stealing and generally unruly behaviour. Initially, virtually anyone could be appointed as a hostel warden or matron, but gradually the service had to be reorganised and staff training provided. More broadly, the contribution of trained staff, including almoners, psychiatric social workers and those involved in childcare and family casework, began to gain official recognition.

During the mid-1940s, social workers were appointed as Ministry of Health regional welfare officers to deal with evacuation problems. Welfare inspectors followed to help with difficult housing cases in the London region. They were appointed because of their knowledge about people in distress, and because they could mobilise statutory and voluntary agencies to address the needs of a particular individual (Titmuss, 1950). Helping homeless people with their personal problems expressed a new view of the relationship between public services and the public served, as the personal social services neared their birth.

The Ministry of Health also encouraged local authorities to employ social workers to develop welfare provision for evacuees and homeless people, as well as matching special needs with special provision. By the end of the war, 70 local authorities had actually done this. Civilian resettlement units, whose staff included social workers, were also established to help returning prisoners of war adjust to freedom in a changed society. Social workers also worked with the Provisional Council for Mental Health (PCMH) and other voluntary organisations. The PCMH developed regional services led by psychiatric social workers. The Citizens' Advice Bureau was established in 1939 and, although largely staffed by volunteers, carried out some casework. In 1940, the Pacifist Service Units, which later became Family Service Units, worked with 'problem' families. Importantly, they worked in teams and carefully recorded their work.

Such developments, culminating in the 1942 Beveridge Report that established the welfare state, confirmed the view that government action rather than inaction was the way forward in terms of addressing social problems. They also heralded what was to come during the social democratic era of the initial postwar years.

Social democracy and the zenith of social work

Social democracy has its origins in Marxism, utopian socialism and a form of revisionism inspired by Engels' later view that evolutionary

—

political action relying on the franchise and parliament was more likely than revolutionary means to favour working-class struggle (Apter, 1993). Early social democrats were committed to the proletariat as the class of the future, believing that it could take economic and political power by such means as universal suffrage, parliamentary democracy and control over the executive branch of government. Once in power, they thought they could eliminate the 'boom and bust' of capitalism by nationalising major industries and planning their subsequent development. The market was therefore rejected as the sole arbiter of justice, and the public favoured over the private sphere. The social democrats also took a strong position on egalitarianism and the need to eliminate the causes of social inequities by state intervention, particularly by the creation of the welfare state. This meant that the market and social justice could coexist. Any social problems that remained could then be explained in terms of an individual's psychological make-up, which was susceptible to diagnosis and treatment by, among others, social workers. Notions of solidarity premised the view that the state could motivate national growth and well-being by the encouragement of social responsibility and the mutuality of social risk (Donzelot, 1979). These social democrats shared an egalitarian, secular and scientific vision of the Enlightenment tradition that corresponded with much of the traditional Labour Party ethos in the form of Fabianism. But how did it relate to the traditional Conservative Party at a time when both major parties were vying for power after the end of the Second World War?

In George and Wilding's (1976) terminology, the traditional Conservative Party consisted of 'anti-collectivists', who are essentially advocates of liberalism, and 'reluctant collectivists'. The reluctant collectivists had similar values to the anti-collectivists, namely liberty, freedom and individualism together with a belief in the free market. However, the reluctants' commitment to these values tended to be conditional and qualified by their intellectual pragmatism. This pragmatism arose from the fact that the free market or capitalism was seen as not being self-regulating; it may be the best economic system, but for it to function efficiently and fairly it required judicious regulation and control. State action, therefore, was accepted as

—

legitimate in certain circumstances, with the extent and nature of this to be determined on the merits of the specific case. The reluctant collectivists also favoured reducing inequalities, although they were not egalitarians, and this separated them from the Fabian socialists. The reluctants, better known as 'One Nation' Conservatives, were to eventually dominate the Conservative Party during the initial postwar period, with similar views also being a force in the Labour Party. To a real extent, there was a convergence of ideas in terms of values and the role of the state in social and economic affairs. One could say that 'the declared policies of the two parties [Labour and Conservative] were agreed on a large number of pressing issues' (Fraser, 1973, p 207).

The Fabian-influenced social reform movement had gathered momentum during the course of the war. It included ideas about improving housing, healthcare and education, as well as ensuring freedom from abject poverty. This was highlighted in the 1942 Beveridge Report (Beveridge, 1942), which argued for the abolishment of the five giants of want, squalor, ignorance, unemployment and ill health, together with the provision of financial security 'from the cradle to the grave'. It captured the imagination of large numbers of the population, especially the working class. Memories of the 1930s and its high levels of unemployment were still fresh in the minds of those once unemployed men and women now fighting for Britain. The sacrifices that people were being asked to make demanded a promise of something better than the pre-war world that had gone before. The idea that winning the war would be rewarded merely by a return to the old days of glaring class inequality and privilege would not have been much of an incentive; instead, the report advocated a postwar Britain driven by welfarist principles, a 'land fit for heroes'. The result was a Labour landslide general election victory in 1945, its manifesto committing it to a radical programme of social and economic reform, including the establishment of the welfare state and the nationalisation of key sections of the economy. This was the social and political landscape on which the social democratic consensus was to be built.

—

The welfare state

The 1944 Education Act had already introduced a comprehensive national education system. Following its general election victory, Labour quickly introduced universal child allowances. Several national insurance/assistance Acts ensued, introducing a system of social insurance that enabled the establishment of unemployment, sickness, maternity, widows, guardians, old-age and funeral benefits, with industrial injuries benefits soon following. The 1946 National Health Service Act led to the National Health Service coming into being in 1948, with improvements to housing occurring after the passing of the 1949 Housing Act. All these developments were the result of a long process beginning with the affirmation of civil rights, through a struggle for political rights, ending with the identification and establishment of social rights (Marshall, 1996 [1950]). They can also be seen as the result of a working-class struggle that culminated in the ruling class having to give concessions in order to preserve the status quo. It is worth noting here that in the 1970s, the balance of power between the classes would change and the gains previously made would in effect be taken away (Ferguson et al, 2002).

The welfare state became an accepted institution, with differences between alternating Labour and Conservative governments during the 1950s, 1960s and into the 1970s amounting to a little more or less government ownership and economic planning. This was based on the ideas of the economist John Maynard Keynes and became known as Keynesianism. It was within this welfare state ideal that modern social work was to become firmly established and it has largely continued to define itself in this context ever since. The 1948 National Assistance Act took the financial care of the poor out of local hands but left local authorities with the responsibility to provide welfare services and residential accommodation for older and disabled people with social care needs. The 1948 Children Act implemented the 1946 Curtis Report on the care of deprived children. Local authority children's departments were established, together with the profession of childcare officer, to provide a secure family environment for children in care. One-year childcare courses were sponsored and financed in 1947 by the Home Office's Central Training Council in Child Care. As well as a focus on fieldwork childcare, courses for residential childcare workers featured from the outset. In the meantime, other local authority officials trained on the job to become the backbone of many health and welfare services.

Seebohm and its aftermath

The separation of child, health and welfare services proved problematic as the postwar years wore on. Although the 1960s in particular were a period of comparative prosperity for social work (Vincent, 1983), concerns emerged about overlapping or gaps in services and departmental rivalries. In the current jargon, demands emerged for a 'one-stop service' focusing on the needs of the whole family. In addition to this, the disparate elements of welfare, mental health, childcare and so on were all identified as carrying out social work. All this led to the 1968 Seebohm Report[1], which established local authority social services departments (SSDs) in 1971, aimed at providing a community-based and family-oriented service available to all. It was an ambitious reorganisation envisaging a comprehensive and universal social work service that included community alternatives to hospitals and other institutions for adults and children. It also envisaged group and community work, as well as casework, approaches to various social problems. The result was intended to be the fifth social service on a par with health, education, income maintenance and housing (Jordan, 2007). The overall aim was that SSDs would enable 'individuals to act reciprocally, giving and receiving services for the well-being of the whole community' (Seebohm Report, 1968, para 2). Ideally, a family or individual would have only one, the so-called 'generic', social worker, although it was also recognised that each social worker, because of temperament or inclination, might be more effective in some fields than others (Leeding, 1976).

The 1960s and 1970s were to be the high watermark of social work. The Council for Training in Social Work was established in 1962 to promote training for social workers in health and welfare services. This resulted in a training explosion, as courses increased in both universities and colleges of further education. The expansion was aided by readily available grants from the three national, publicly

SOCIAL WORK

financed training councils covering probation, childcare and now health and welfare. The National Institute of Social Work was established in 1961, aimed at achieving excellence in practice and management in social work. Another important factor to consider is that although social workers already had considerable power in relation to people with mental health difficulties following the 1959 Mental Health Act, this was to be extended to other service-user areas. The 1969 Children and Young Persons Act gave social workers increased authority and influence by removing responsibility for the disposal of convicted young offenders from the police and magistrates and giving it to them instead. The Act also enabled social workers to remove children from their parents on emergency protection orders with little right of challenge, and then to seek care orders. The 1970 Chronically Sick and Disabled Persons Act placed the onus on local authorities to identify the needs of the sick and disabled people, so opening up a new area of professional competence for social work. Also in 1970, the British Association of Social Workers was formed by bringing together medical social workers, psychiatric social workers, childcare officers, moral welfare officers and others (but not probation officers). In 1971, the Central Council for the Education and Training in Social Work (CCETSW) superseded the training councils for childcare, probation and social work. Its functions included developing education and training to meet the needs of the personal social services, ensuring the quality of such education and training, and providing bursaries for social work students. CCETSW's initial challenge was to unify over 120 courses, which eventually resulted in a generic Certificate of Qualification in Social Work. It also introduced the Certificate in Social Service (CSS) for staff other than social workers. Post-qualifying courses also emerged.

It is perhaps difficult to understand the sense of optimism as the new SSDs were established and staffed by enthusiastic, newly qualified social workers. There was a strong element of idealism, with staff being fully committed to what they were doing (Ivory, 2005). There was a feeling that this was the brink of a new era, with real money to spend; indeed, spending increased by10% a year in real terms for the first few years. Even more notable was the relative autonomy that social workers could bring to their practice. When first starting social work after qualifying, I was struck by the fact that I was actively encouraged to pursue my interest areas – work with juvenile offenders, and group and community work, for example. And it was not just individual social workers who had this relative autonomy; the team itself could largely prioritise which problems to tackle in its area and how it was going to deal with them. Weekly team meetings enabled new referrals to be freely discussed and allocated. There was also an element of peer/group supervision as suggestions for dealing with cases were debated. Working generically, I recall dealing with people with mental health issues, learning difficulties and physical difficulties as well as with older people and children and families. I was also involved with assessing prospective foster and adoptive carers. It really was an exhilarating time as I took to being a caseworker with a community orientation.

The growing self-confidence of social work was also evident in the considerable advances in social work theory and practice over this period[2]. During the 1950s and the 1960s, Freudian-based concepts were incorporated into mainstream casework (Halmos, 1965), with psychology being a major component of social work training. Psycho-analytical concepts such as early family experiences, unconscious motivation, defence mechanisms and the powerful drives of sex and aggression were all influential. It took Wootton (1959) to make the key point that social work was concentrating on theories of intra-or, at best, inter-psychic processes rather than the economic and political sources of problems. She did not want social workers posing as miniature psychoanalysts or psychiatrists, and such comments were repeated by the radical theorists and practitioners of the 1970s. This was reinforced as sociology, particularly from a Marxist perspective, became increasingly influential, not least in terms of explaining the structural causes of poverty and bad housing. This involved a move from focusing on private troubles to public issues (Bailey and Brake, 1975). Social administration, social policy and political theory were other key subject areas for study.

Nevertheless, casework remained the main method in social work, enabling a systematic approach to practice and helping to unify internally an occupational group located in a variety of settings with diverse roles and responsibilities (Parton, 1996b). It also provided an internally coherent knowledge base derived from psychodynamic theory and psychology, this being a focus for professionalisation and legitimating its location in the 'psy' complex. Its distinctive contribution was the claim that is was concerned with the whole person, and with providing personal skills in human relationships and an understanding of individuals and families. It also provided a method for assessment and intervention and legitimated social work, helping it overcome its essential ambiguities.

Initially, casework focused on individual pathology rather than strengths, with a tendency to be overly non-directive and to overestimate the power of the casework relationship itself, thereby neglecting environmental factors (Younghusband, 1981). Things gradually changed and, instead of concentrating on childhood experiences, for instance, more was made of the individual's current situation and of reinforcing their capacity to cope and the strength of their support systems. Long-term casework was often preferred, but the development of task-centred casework in the 1970s showed that time-limited work was feasible. The earlier tendency of casework to treat the client as separate from their family so as to enable unhurried and uninterrupted sessions began to be superseded by discussions with the family as a whole, with family therapy becoming more common. Crisis intervention and behaviour modification techniques also flourished, with positive, rather than negative, reinforcement being favoured, particularly as far as children were concerned.

Although casework was the dominant method, as it is even more so today albeit in a more limited form, group and community work gradually (re-)gained in importance. I recall once writing an essay during the mid-1970s about the need for 'a community orientation for the caseworker'; the focus should not just be the individual concerned, but their relationship with the rest of the family, employment or school and the neighbourhood as a whole. Group work was of particular significance in work with young offenders on intermediate treatment schemes, while community work involved working alongside local people on issues defined by them. There was also considerable interest in the integrated method – the flexible use of casework, group and community work – and the related unitary model based on systems theory. These methods and models appealed

—

to the more radical social workers who were also influenced by the establishment of 12 community development projects (CDPs) in 1969 by the Home Office in areas of multiple deprivation. These projects consisted of field and research workers, with community workers having a significant role. They had a dual responsibility to both local people and the local authority, which eventually led to various tensions and difficulties. In particular, their findings tended to argue for multi-deprivation to be redefined and reinterpreted in terms of structural constraints rather than psychological motivations. Social malaise should not be explained in terms of personal deficiencies but as the product of external pressures arising from wider society (Bailey and Brake, 1975). It is perhaps not surprising that the CDPs were wound up by the government during the 1970s.

Social care

Throughout this chapter, little has been said of social care, a form of care that developed from residential, day and other group care (Payne, 2009). During the 19th century, little of importance occurred in this area, with individuals relying on family and friends for support. In the 1930s, social care initiatives occurred in charitable organisations such as the Caldecott Community, National Children's Home and Dr Barnado's, the latter introducing new training schemes for staff. However, until the establishment of the welfare state, comparatively little progress was made. From the 1950s to the 1970s there was increasing recognition of the importance of providing services designed to support people so that they could maintain their independence and play as full a part in society as possible. It involved direct practical support to individuals in need and included, for example, providing accommodation; help with washing, dressing, feeding, shopping and cleaning; meals on wheels, and so on. Children, young and old people, and people with learning, physical and mental health difficulties all used these services and their increasing importance began to be recognised in the postwar period when it was realised that staff needed to be adequately trained; the above comments in relation to CSS are evidence of this.

—

In many ways, social care, like social work, was coming of age as the social democratic settlement imbued the economic, political and social spheres with an air of confidence. The 'five giants' really did appear to be in the process of being vanquished by the creation of the welfare state. One biography refers to the postwar years up to 1951 as 'the age of optimism' and the period 1951-74 as 'consolidation' (Timmins, 1996). The National Health Service, a new tripartite system of secondary education, and income maintenance and social services systems were all established and higher education expanded. There were considerable improvements in housing, and employment was high. Although poverty may not have gone away, the 1950s and 1960s saw a real material improvement in people's lives following an unprecedented period of economic growth. 'You've never had it so good', crowed prime minister Harold Macmillan and to an extent he was right, as living standards rose for almost everyone. The working class could begin to dream of a better life for themselves and their children than their own parents could have ever imagined. In explaining this sense of optimism, of how all things could be improved for all people and thus for society as a whole, and in turn how it affected social work, two other factors need to be considered, namely the influence of the counterculture and the New Left during the late 1960s and early 1970s.

The counterculture and the New Left

Tierney (1996) looks at the counterculture and the New Left in relation to developments in criminology, but his comments are equally valid in relation to what happened in social work. The counterculture represented disengagement with the values of mainstream, conformist culture, and an attempt to create a non-materialistic, more expressive and meaningful alternative. It primarily emanated from middle-class youth, especially the increasing numbers of students of the time. The emphasis was on personal liberation from the constraints imposed by a dehumanised consumer society, where *things* had become more important than people. It arose not from material hardship, but from a feeling that affluence in itself was not personally fulfilling (Pearson, 1975)[3]. Resistance entailed questioning dominant ideas in relation to such things as sexuality, drug use and appropriate styles of dress. It involved the rejection of consumerism and conventional mores together with a commitment to cultural diversity and a sympathetic, even celebratory, approach to deviancy. Ultimately, the counterculture was a critique of, and reaction to, consumer society, although this was abstracted from its economic and political structures.

The New Left also questioned soul-destroying consumerism, although here the target was a specifically capitalist society. Long-established groups such as the Communist Party were seen as ossified because their formulations and strategies had ceased to provided a meaningful alternative vision. Instead, the New Left drew on the critical theory of the Frankfurt School. For example, Marcuse (1964) saw capitalist societies as one-dimensional because important social and political questions were relegated to second place behind questions about the best soap powder or cigarette to use, something that The Rolling Stones' classic song 'Satisfaction' refers to. The Frankfurt School argued that humankind's relationship to nature, which grew out of the Enlightenment, was not fulfilling real social progress. As humans had manipulated nature, so those with power now used technology, including the media, to manipulate the less powerful, not just at a physical level but also at the level of consciousness and the senses. Social order, therefore, depended not only on overt measures of social control but on concentrating people's minds on an overriding concern with consumer goods[4].

There were points of fusion between the counterculture and the New Left, with many students as well as the wider public becoming influenced by their ideas. Advocates may not all have been drop-outs high on drugs, listening to The Rolling Stones in hippy communes, but students did have more opportunities than those in paid employment to experiment with such different ideas and lifestyles. Indeed, in Chapter One I hinted at this in relation to my own biography. Furthermore, social work itself appealed to those who wanted to distance themselves from the worst excesses of consumerist/capitalist society. It might have been too bold a step to opt out of society totally, but by doing social work you could, at least to some extent, shun these excesses by not being directly involved in the exploitative and/or consumer-oriented process. At the same time, one could attempt to work with and alleviate the problems and difficulties that afflicted the casualties of an unfair and unjust system. Finally, by adopting what was to become the radical/critical social work perspective, the possibility of being 'in and [yet] against the state' became a reality (London Edinburgh Weekend Return Group, 1980). For many young graduates, social work became an ethical career in which to engage with capitalist society.

Conclusion

After a hundred years of, at times, slow progress, by the early 1970s social work had finally arrived as a profession or, perhaps more appropriately for some, a semi-profession. In essence, it was a social democratic response to the social problems of the time that involved the creation of the welfare state. Such a situation ought to be seen within the context of state *administration* of public services including social work (Harris and White, 2009a), which provides a secure and positive basis from which to practice. It was founded in part on respect for professionalism, including its knowledge base and the identification of what was considered professionally correct practice. Administration and professionalism coexisted through structures that had a degree of bureaucratic hierarchy with rules and procedures within and through which professionalism operated. By such measures, an administrative system was conducive to social workers being accorded areas of discretion within their practice, with clients and users thereby benefiting from their expertise. Such views are certainly borne out by the earlier comments in relation to my induction to practice as a newly qualified social worker.

As Jordan (2007) points out, it was not only in social work that this period can be seen as the high point of collectivism led by an organising state. As we have seen, major developments also occurred in relation to health, housing, income maintenance and education. Arguably, it was Britain's attempt to emulate countries such as Sweden, by developing public infrastructures and services to shape the context of citizens' lives and their interactions with each other from the cradle to the grave. The election of Margaret Thatcher as prime minister, however, meant that Keynesianism was to be replaced by monetarism, the welfare state was to come under attack and neoliberalism was to emerge with a vengeance as a successor to social democracy. The consequences of this Thatcherite revolution on social work and on society as a whole are still being felt today.

Notes

[1] The Kilbrandon Report (1965) laid a similar basis for social work in Scotland.

[2] See Payne (2005b) for a discussion of the social work theories and methods referred to here, as well as many others.

[3] Much of this remains current; witness concerns about the fact that although living standards have risen, this has not led to an increase in happiness and well-being; see Jordan (2007, 2008) and Chapter Seven for a discussion.

[4] Again this resonates with the situation today.

THREE

Thatcherism: opportunities and challenges

The seeds of Margaret Thatcher's general election success in 1979 were laid in the early 1970s by the world economic crisis of 1973. This crisis was activated by a sharp rise in oil prices, but it also reflected much deeper structural problems in the British economy. These included a steady decline in the country's share of the world export of manufactured goods, along with falling investment and productivity, and rising inflation (Harman, 1984; Ferguson, 2008). The crisis had three main consequences. First, it led to the return of mass unemployment, which reached a total of one million in 1979, higher than it had been since the Great Depression of the 1930s. Second, it led to attacks on the welfare state, particularly after the International Monetary Fund pressed Britain to reduce public spending. This resulted in the closure of schools and hospitals, and the targeting, or more appropriately rationing, of social work and social services to particular user groups. Within a few years of the Seebohm Report (1968), the selective mentality of the Poor Law had come to prevail over the universalist aspirations of the report's more radical proponents (Langan, 1993). Third, and most significantly, the economic crisis led to the end of the social democratic consensus. The centrality of Keynesianism, an acceptance of the key role of the state in the management of essential industries, in managing and regulating the economy, and in the provision of welfare, was to end. Monetarism, the forerunner of today's neoliberalism, was to be its replacement, even though this change began with public expenditure cuts introduced by the Labour government of 1974-79 (Kerr, 1981). In practical terms, this meant a return to the free market ideology that had been discarded after the Great Depression, albeit adapted to the globalised world of the 1980s and 1990s.

—

The sea change in the ideological climate occurred because during the 1970s neither the Conservative nor Labour governments seemed able to solve the economic problems facing Britain. Consequently, both saw an increase in political activity from their radical wings. Within Labour, the socialist left was organising, while, more significantly for the purposes of this chapter, the New Right was in the ascendency in the Conservative Party. Both rejected the postwar acceptance of the coexistence of the Keynesian welfare state and advanced capitalism, with the New Right arguing for a complete break with Keynesianism because social democracy was seen to be prefigurative of socialism itself. As we shall see, the New Right saw the welfare state and in turn social work as part of the problem.

I begin this chapter by outlining neoliberal philosophy or ideology, including the work of two key thinkers, namely Hayek and Friedman (see O'Brien and Penna, 1998). The former was a lifelong opponent of the social and economic doctrines influencing social democracy, while the latter's formulation of monetary theory was a formative influence in New Right economic policy. This is followed by a discussion of some of the policy developments of the Thatcher and Major years, especially as they affected social work. Although in many ways social work continued to progress in relation to areas such as community social work, work with young offenders and anti-oppressive practice, it had to cope with continued rationing of services. There were also changes in relation to the move from child welfare to child protection, and challenges in the form of the development of care management with older people and the withdrawal of the necessity for probation officers to have a social work qualification. Such developments amounted to increased questioning of the value of social work, particularly because of perceived failures in relation to child abuse and, to a lesser extent, its concern with social justice and social change.

Neoliberalism

As well as containing a critique of the postwar social democratic consensus, neoliberalism is a political and economic approach that has been adopted throughout most of the countries in the world to address the crisis of profitability exposed by the economic crisis of 1973. It is a theory of political economic practices based on the belief in individual freedom and of liberating individual entrepreneurial skills within an institutional framework characterised by strong property rights (Harvey, 2005). In short, it is the belief that free markets and free trade will best achieve human well-being.

Hayek and freedom

Hayek's prolific writings amount to a concern to construct a philosophy of *freedom* by restating and reformulating classical liberalism. As we saw in Chapter Two, this is seen in negative terms as the absence of coercion on the private activities of individuals. By coercion, Hayek means the control of the environment or circumstances of one individual by another so that he/she is forced to serve the ends of others (Hayek, 1960). This negative concept of freedom sees the collectivist state planning of the Fabians as misconceived and the welfare state as opposed to individual freedom.

He bases his theory of knowledge on a critique of French Enlightenment rationalism, which resulted in political structures inspired by ideals of social justice and equality. It is an attack on the concept of reason as a basis for understanding the world, arguing that we can never fully understand the world because it is impossible to totally grasp the innumerable details it comprises. Instead, knowledge is an evolutionary phenomenon characterised by fragmentation rather than coherence, with 'tacit' knowledge being the most important thing, something that develops during the evolutionary process in the course of human cultural practice. All social life, Hayek argues, depends on this tacit knowledge, which manifests itself in social and moral rules, customs and norms that are transmitted by churches, families and other institutions. Like many postmodernists, he is also against the view of science as a progressive force that can understand and thus eradicate social problems. As the evolutionary process is a continuous adaptation to unforeseen and unpredictable events, this leads to a critique of the historicism of Comte and Marx, the belief that there is an overall pattern to history or laws governing its progress (Hayek, 1982).

—

The notion of 'tradition' is important because it transmits the 'successful' cultural norms and rules through each generation, thereby ensuring the best conditions for the promotion of human reproduction and welfare. Hayek favours the 'spontaneous order' of the liberal 18th century (as opposed to 'constructivist', state-directed society), which embodies a set of 'commercial morals' sustained by a process of socialisation in the family, community and economic life. These 'morals' become geared to the functioning of the small enterprise in a competitive market economy upheld by a limited state structure. However, the shift in social thought by the French Enlightenment disturbed the delicate and spontaneous balance between tacit knowledge, social institutions and markets, leading to attempts to plan modern societies and to control the distribution of income and wealth for political purposes. Inspired by French concepts of liberty, which include equality and social justice, the liberal notion of freedom was, he argues, slowly displaced (Hayek, 1960, 1982).

Hayek is a micro-economist who is against the methodology of macro-economics, particularly the notion of economics being a predictive, objective science that is a force for progress. Again it is an attack on the French Enlightenment, with its critique of macro-economics making a distinction between the economy and the market. The former is a set of deliberately coordinated actions designed with particular goals in mind, whereas the latter refers to numerous interrelated economies in which individuals pursue their own ends. These may be selfish and private, but overall, Hayek argues, they result in the increased well-being of all. As a corollary, central state planning will always be inefficient compared with market processes because there is no mechanism to compensate for the role played by the prices and wages system combined with competition. These are seen as the mechanisms that coordinate the myriad of activities making up an economy, feeding information to producers, consumers and resource owners that indicates needs, preferences and availability. Competition is also the key element in the market process, as it encourages the development of new products and lowers costs owing to the need for efficient production.

Hayek (1960) acknowledges that inequality follows logically from his view of the minimalist state, with market processes resulting in unpredictable and unequal material outcomes, but argues that the overall benefit outweighs individual disadvantages. Attempts by the state to remedy disadvantages are seen as coercive, restricting individual freedom and leading to a decline in individual responsibility. The only equality Hayek favours is the *formal* – equality before the law. In addition, substantive or material inequalities in the market are not morally unjust because injustice requires an outcome to be intended, whereas market outcomes are unintended consequences of impersonal processes. Not surprisingly, Hayek is against the notion of socioeconomic rights, as these can only exist in a society totally directed and administered by the state. To the extent that he sees the need, for example, for poverty to be addressed, he advocates allowing the accumulation of aggregate wealth to 'trickle down' to those in the lower socioeconomic groups.

Hayek sees the welfare state as leading to increased regulation of citizens, increased taxation and distortion of market processes, and the gradual erosion of liberty. He does not advocate the complete removal of the state from welfare activities, but rather suggests that any intervention should be strictly minimal and not involve a monopoly on services. A monopoly would increase the centralised power of the state and discourage private and charitable provision, which actually should be encouraged. Finally, he advocates state withdrawal from interference in economic processes such as income policies, minimum wage laws and employment protection legislation, all of which would reduce the power of trade unions in economic and political life.

Friedman and free markets

Friedman, like Hayek, sees liberty as being best secured through the market, with state intervention harming both economic growth and individual freedom. His work, a detailed empirical examination of monetary policy in the US, undermined Keynesian economics and the intellectual and moral legitimacy of state intervention in the economy over the postwar years (Green, 1979). He reinterprets the causes of the 1929-33 depression, arguing that the stock market slump was worsened by the state intervention of the Federal Reserve System. It was therefore the government, rather than the market, that caused the resulting depression (Friedman, 1962); no doubt he would have employed similar arguments regarding the 2008-10 recession caused by the banking sector. His political critique of the US extended to the postwar welfare state in Britain and elsewhere.

Keynesianism was therefore seen to have failed in postwar Britain because of the combination of increasing inflation and unemployment, both of which challenged the assumptions of postwar economics. The appearance of stagflation in the 1970s – a stagnant economy with high inflation – should not have occurred according to Keynes's general theory. So if the theories on which his demand management was based were seriously flawed, all the assumptions of the state management of the economy with resulting growth and full employment collapsed. Consequently, the economic problems of the 1970s were not the result of capitalism itself but of Keynesianism, the political administration of capitalism. Friedman saw inflation as being linked to the amount of money circulating in the economy, so it was this that needed to be controlled rather than the activities of business. Overall, it was high inflation, rising unemployment, a large publicly managed and financed sector of the economy increasingly absorbing more of the gross domestic product, and low economic growth that exposed Keynesian economic policy. Two policy priorities gained political significance from these circumstances: controlling the money supply and creating wealth through tax incentives. All this required more investment, achieved by cutting taxes and public spending, and reducing unemployment by cutting wages and benefits, the latter through establishing an absolute concept of need.

Monetarism is often presented as a technical solution to economic problems, but in fact it involves transforming the political institutions and social rights of the postwar period. Friedman (1962) and Friedman and Friedman (1980) argue that socialist political and economic structures undermine and eventually lead to the abolition of individual liberty. One example is the gradually expanding meanings ascribed to equality – not only equality before the law, but equality of opportunity and of outcome. Equality of outcome is seen as particularly problematic in a number of areas. First, inequality is an inevitable outcome of markets, but less so than under other systems. Free markets also increase overall social wealth and this ultimately

—

benefits the poor. On the other hand, an emphasis on material justice leads to the problem of an extended state apparatus directing the activities of individuals in the market (by, for instance, minimum wages, protective legislation and prices policy) and through the tax system in order to equalise income distribution. Second, extensive state welfare has created a class of bureaucrats who have a vested interest in expanding state intervention. This benefits powerful producer groups at the expense of consumers who come to depend on the continuing provision of services, losing individual initiative and personal responsibility in the process. And third, social insurance is seen as a tax on employment, thus generating unemployment and fostering socialism by raising taxation without public debate. By paying taxes for benefits, people are deprived of making their own arrangements in the market and have no choice but to take what the state offers. Choice in welfare, by contrast, will increase personal liberty and strengthen social and community bonds, while minimal social security provision will encourage employment and add to personal savings and security. Traditional forms of welfare support, such as the family, voluntary sector and the market, would also flourish, again reviving individual initiative and responsibility.

Hayek and Friedman provide the political philosophy or ideological background to neoliberalism and the New Right in particular. Their arguments centre on the primacy of individual freedom and economic prosperity, and have had considerable influence on political, economic and social welfare theory including social work.

Social work under Thatcherism

During the early 1970s, many members of the Conservative Party, including Margaret Thatcher and Keith Joseph, took up neoliberal ideas. They became an influential grouping that broke with the 'One Nation' Toryism of the 'wet' wing of the party and formed the New Right. They went on to win the general election of 1979 with arguments centring on the so-called dependency culture, whereby large sections of the population had become lazy and undisciplined on the back of a too-generous welfare state, and on militant trade unions holding employers and governments to ransom. In addition,

—

the nation was being 'swamped' by immigrants, there was anarchy in schools, with parents abrogating their responsibilities, and a lack of law and order in wider society. The New Right was also concerned about state intervention and wanted to curtail its activities in three areas. This involved reducing the scope of services, some or all of which would be privatised; cutting the level of state benefits to a minimum, leaving individuals to make provision for themselves if they so wished; and introducing privately (rather than government) administered and managed services (Hay, 1996). There was a desire to roll back the state and in the process weaken the trade unions and local government, and to ensure that nationalised industries were privatised together with parts of the welfare state, which in any case needed to be dismantled. In practical terms, the early Thatcher years saw a number of initiatives quickly introduced: restrictions on picketing, abolition of trades union closed shops and an insistence on private ballots; cuts in welfare benefits; the selling off of council houses; support for private schools; and the introduction of charges for certain social services, notably those that affected the care of elderly people and those with special needs (Taylor-Gooby, 1981). 'Progress' was made in all of these areas by the Conservative governments of the 1980s and 1990s, and, as we shall see in the next chapter, continued under New Labour. Social work, too, was eventually to experience fundamental changes.

Professional social work's emergence in the late 1960s and early 1970s coincided with the social democratic project coming under considerable pressure. The economic difficulties, together with a perceived growth in social disorder and indiscipline, undermined the economic and social pillars of welfarism, and the political consensus that supported it (Parton, 1996b). Being part and parcel of the welfarist project, social work was to come under attack both from the left and, most importantly, from the right. Even at its peak, social work was contested and subject to a wide variety of public, political and professional debate and debasement often in the full glare of publicity (Aldridge, 1994). Around this time the left, including feminists and anti-racists, and a variety of user groups and other professional and community interests were concerned that social services departments were costly, ineffective, distant and oppressive, leaving the user powerless and without a voice. For some of these critics, social work was seen as an element of class control, preserving the status quo of capitalist societies by controlling and regulating the working class. Such critics, however coherent their arguments might have been, often failed to develop constructive alternatives. Unwittingly such groups did open up a political space that was to be colonised by the Thatcherite New Right.

Drawing on neoliberalism, the New Right espoused a number of themes. As alluded to above, it was against public expenditure on state welfare, promoting instead an increased emphasis on self-help and family support. The focus was on individual responsibility, 'choice' and freedom, together with an extension of the commodification of social relations. Such notions resulted in a move away from the certainties associated with a professionally driven, local authority controlled system of social work and social services. More specifically, challenges and uncertainties arose from changes introduced by the 1989 Children Act, the 1990 National Health Service and Community Care Act and the 1991 Criminal Justice Act, as well as changes in social work training introduced by the Diploma in Social Work in 1989 (see Chapter Five). The reader will note that these developments occurred some ten years or more after Thatcher's first general election victory. This is largely because, despite a growing questioning of social work during her time in office, she had more pressing problems to address in the early years of her premiership, including the Falklands War of 1982, clashes with trade unions following the miners' strike of 1984-85 and the various privatisations of nationalised industries. Admittedly, social work was affected by moves away from genericism, with separate teams being formed for specific user groups such as children and families (with further sub-divisions subsequently taking place in relation to fostering/adoption and young offenders), elderly people, those with mental health issues and so on. However, other than focusing on their particular user group, social workers in these teams saw little change in their day-to-day work as the 1980s progressed. Moreover, with the publication of the Barclay Report (1982), which advocated community social work, it was still possible to develop a progressive, even radical/critical practice.

—

Community social work

The Barclay Committee was set up in 1980 to look at the role and tasks of social workers. It was a period when the new Thatcher government seemed committed to achieving cutbacks in social services as well as challenging much of what social workers did (Jordan and Parton, 1983). The then Secretary of State for Health and Social Security, Sir Keith Joseph, had been heavily involved in the publicisation of the Maria Colwell child abuse case (Secretary of State for Social Services, 1974). The Conservatives had also long been concerned by the liberal intentions of the 1969 Children and Young Persons Act. Other attacks centred on so-called 'scroungers' and 'layabouts', whom social workers were seen as supporting and encouraging. Right-wing critiques also questioned the effectiveness of social work and the shortcomings of its professional skills (Brewer and Lait, 1980). It is in this context that the Barclay Report (1982) was published.

For many, the report amounted to a defence of social work (Jordan and Parton, 1983) or more appropriately 'community social work', something that is subject to various interpretations that can be used to support both the political left and right. On the one hand, it can be used to challenge and improve the way local authority social services are delivered, and on the other, it can amount to actually reducing these services, leaving people to rely on the voluntary, informal and private sectors (Beresford and Croft, 1984). At its heart lies the decentralisation and debureaucratisation of services, designed to enable social workers to build and maintain closer links with other agencies and the local community. The actual influence of community social work on practice during the 1980s was variable, but there were a few areas where it made an impact, such as in Normanton, West Yorkshire (Cooper, 1983). Another example is the community social work I undertook with colleagues and referred to in the introduction (Rogowski and Harrison, 1992).

During 1986, there was a review of social work services for children and families in Oldham carried out by a working group involving social workers, managers and the academic Bill Jordan. It drew on the town's 1970s community development project, as well as the Barclay Report's advocacy of community social work. The group came out in favour of a decentralised, locally based service that envisaged some devolution of power and responsibility to social workers. Such a move was seen to have several advantages, including greater accessibility for residents, other workers/professionals, community groups and organisations. It could lead to the breakdown of the traditional relationship between social workers and users, with the former becoming more approachable and more able to develop flexible responses to local needs and problems. Finally, it enabled greater understanding of the community, including its problems, needs and strengths.

These changes envisaged a change in style of social work with a focus on people defining and meeting their own needs as opposed to having them defined and met by 'experts'. People were seen as having strengths and lacking power rather than having individual or family defects. There was less preoccupation with a close-knit, inward-looking, office-based team and more emphasis on going out into the community, meeting a wider range of people, getting to know and strengthening networks, and starting and supporting community groups. This could lead to a less defensive, crisis-oriented role and a more proactive, preventative one in which casework was integrated with more informal, group and community work.

Our small team on on the most deprived estate in Oldham (see Rogowski and Harrison, 1992) tried to work informally with people without having to take formal referrals, although when referrals were taken they were dealt with along community social work lines. There was less emphasis on intra- or inter-psychic processes and more of a focus on problems and difficulties defined by the user, which were then related to the wider context of the neighbourhood and society. A single parent with three children, one of whom was accommodated on a long-term basis, comes to mind. She was lacking in confidence, was lonely and isolated, and the only contacts she had with people were largely negative. She also had housing and financial problems, and her relationship with her ex-husband was characterised by drunkenness and domestic violence. She had a distrust of health visitors and social workers as a result of her first child being removed, and no contact with school in respect of her eldest child. Neighbours made allegations about her lack of care of the children, including

—

her leaving them unsupervised. On one occasion, while in a temper, she threw a shoe at one of her daughters, causing a black eye and resulting in the children being placed on the (then) child protection register. Rather than dealing with the issues solely in terms of the mother's parenting, we focused on the issues she identified as being problematic and on her social networks, which led to attempts being made to develop and strengthen those more positive ones.

Childcare places were arranged for her youngest child and the (then) social services hierarchy was made aware of the need for more such places. Contact was made with the (then) Department of Social Security, energy companies and housing department so as to address the family's financial and housing problems. Discussions with the health visitor and teachers at the children's school ensured that they had a fuller, more sympathetic understanding of the mother's predicament, and she in turn began to have more trust and confidence in them. The social worker was already in contact with some of the neighbours, some of whom were having similar problems to the mother, and gradually both they and she began to offer mutual understanding and support rather than hostility and anger. Contact was also made with a local community centre and the mother eventually helped with the playgroup there, later becoming involved with young people who were solvent users (see below). I could go on, but suffice to say that the mother's confidence increased, her drinking decreased, her relationship with her ex-husband improved, her children were removed from the child protection register and she certainly became a valuable member of the local community.

Looking more specifically at group and community work issues, there were a number of projects that we were involved with. First, we helped support a women's refuge that was in danger of being closed down. A colleague was co-opted on to the management committee and a new constitution including manager–workers and workers–residents agreements helped ensure its survival. Second, we were involved in setting up and running an estate forum that included representatives of various agencies that covered the estate together with local residents. Third, we were involved with a single parents' group and with a group of parents who were having problems dealing with their children's challenging behaviour. Fourth, and perhaps most significantly in that the work has continued to the present day, we helped set up a project for youths who used solvents.

The local community's concerns about solvent users was well known but specifically arose following our involvement in a survey of the needs and problems of a particular estate and discussions with the local tenants' association. Many residents simply wanted the youths moved away by the police, but following a public meeting it was agreed that a more constructive strategy was required and eventually it was decided a group work response was the way forward (Rogowski et al, 1989). The group met weekly and was staffed by a local community worker, residents/volunteers and social workers. It provided recreational activities as well as advice and information about solvents, welfare rights and housing issues. By involving local residents, the group helped break down barriers, which resulted in residents gaining some understanding of the pressures facing young people who are often forced to lead bored, aimless lives with little hope for the future. Perhaps it is not surprising why some people take to solvents to briefly escape reality. There is an obvious economic and political dimension here that relates to radical social work's concern with conscientisation and politicisation. Linked to this is the fact that the residents were also able to share their experience with local schools and parents. As for parents of solvent users, we were able to put some of them in contact with each other so they could talk through the problems and difficulties of bringing up youngsters in deprived areas, and discuss possible ways forward. The success of this project can be gauged by the fact that a local vicar took a keen interest. He wanted to put it on a more secure financial footing, and pursued it with his hierarchy. Eventually, the Church of England provided funding for a fully staffed, permanent project. It continued for a number of years, turning out to be the precursor of part of the current statutory service for solvent and other drug users.

The point has also to be made that while pursuing such community social work we were able to represent people in a variety of ways, not least in relation to welfare rights and housing issues. I can well recall, for example, accompanying parents to various social security tribunals helping to put their case for a financial/benefit payment. It is sad to say that few social workers are involved in such activity today.

—

A question that emerges is whether community social work is compatible with social work's statutory role, especially in the field of child protection/safeguarding. One view is that you can become too close to local people, thereby being unable to adopt a child-focused approach and in turn failing to recognise and identify dangers to children. My retort is simply that proximity to the community, and to people with problems, means that there was no need to overreact to situations and that genuinely serious problems, like child abuse, soon emerge naturally from the plethora of minor difficulties.

Social work, young offenders and the successful revolution

The intention of the 1969 Children's and Young Persons Act was that the vast majority of juvenile offenders would be dealt with in the community by intermediate treatment. Although only partially implemented, it became the scapegoat for the perceived ills of young offending and youth justice in the 1970s. With the breakdown of the social democratic consensus, there was a move towards 'law and order' authoritarianism (Hall et al, 1978). The 1982 Criminal Justice Act resulted in an increased focus on detention centres and the introduction of experimental 'short, sharp, shock' regimes, although there was a pragmatic and financial interest in keeping young offenders out of custody wherever possible. Nevertheless, the 1982 Act amounted to a move away from a concern with the welfare and/or treatment of young offenders back towards punishment (Gelsthorpe and Morris, 1994). Children and young people in trouble with the law were, and certainly still are, seen first and foremost as *offenders* who needed controlling and punishing, rather than adolescents facing problems and difficulties requiring help and support. The New Right simply argued that welfare/treatment approaches to young offenders did not prevent or act as a deterrent to offending and nor did they lead to successful rehabilitation. However, the financial interest in keeping young offenders out of custody whenever possible coincided with David Thorpe and his colleagues' work at Lancaster University, who wanted to deal with youth crime more humanely and effectively, and their views went on to dominate social work with young offenders for a time (Thorpe et al, 1980). They were influenced by labelling theories (Becker, 1963; Schur, 1973) as well as the 'nothing works' thesis (Martinson, 1974) and developed an administrative criminology aimed at systems and youth crime management (Pitts, 1988). This takes the view that acts that can be labelled as criminal are normal during adolescence and not precursors to adult crime – most young people literally grow out of it – and that intervention designed to prevent such acts is simply not possible. However, it may be possible to do something about the consequences of such acts and that is to lengthen the route to custody and to create various diversions along the way by utilising 'ordinary' supervision orders as well as those with intermediate treatment and specified activity components. In this scenario, systems management and monitoring strategies are also devised to keep young people out of the youth justice system whenever possible. These can highlight the way in which young black people can become victims of racism in the system and reveal inconsistencies in the treatment of young women compared with that of young men (Blagg and Smith, 1989). Along with all of this, genuine alternatives to incarceration or intensive intermediate treatment schemes are developed for heavy-end or persistent offenders.

The rationale for this 'new orthodoxy' was that there was no evidence that early social work intervention had any positive effect in terms of preventing or reducing youth crime but rather had the effect of 'up-tariffing' young people when they do offend and hastening their incarceration (Blagg and Smith, 1989).

In fact, during the 1980s there was a significant and sustained decline in recorded crime by young people and a decline in the number receiving custodial sentences. As Farrington and Langan (1992) note, several factors help explain the 'successful revolution' (Jones, 1989, 1993). First, there were demographic changes in that there was an 18% drop in the population of 14- to 16-year-old males in the period 1981 to 1988. Second, the 1982 Criminal Justice Act introduced community service to 16-year-olds and contrary to some expectations this was used as an alternative to incarceration. The 1982 Act also introduced restrictions on the use of custody as well as another non-custodial sentence, the supervision order with specified activities. Third, the growth of intensive intermediate treatment and the change in practice as Thorpe and colleagues' work became the 'new orthodoxy' meant there was effective offence-focused work with 'heavy-end' or persistent offenders. And fourth, diversion from court by cautioning, again linked to the 'new orthodoxy', led to a decline in the number of young offenders being formally processed.

So successful was this revolution that the Home Office (1988) signalled its intention to transfer lessons from youth justice to policies in relation to offenders more generally. The Green Paper recognised that most young offenders grow out of crime as they mature and that they need help and encouragement to become law abiding, arguing that even a short spell in custody was likely to have a deleterious effect by confirming them as criminals, particularly as they learn skills from other offenders. Despite this endorsement for perhaps the most significant ever evidence-based social work success, from 1991 onwards there was a noticeable change in official attitude towards young offenders and youth crime in general, as 'populist punitiveness' (Bottoms, 1995) emerged. This can be traced to a number of urban disturbances in 1991 that featured young men in confrontations with the police, and the murder of two-year-old James Bulger after he was abducted and killed by two ten-year-old boys. Long-standing concerns about young offenders became distorted and exaggerated in the mass media, with discourses being about individuals terrorising communities, and the police and courts being powerless to deal with them. 'Persistent young offenders' became the moral panic of the day, with politicians of all parties becoming increasingly punitive in their pronouncements (Hagell and Newburn, 1994).

Such punitiveness is evident in the legal framework for the adjudication of young offenders that existed during the 1990s, largely in the 1991 Criminal Justice Act, which reflected punishment by introducing community penalties. The court orders available were not there to help young people who had social problems and had offended, but instead were to offer punishment and control in the community (Stewart et al, 1994). Noticeably, the evidence from the 'successful revolution' of the 1980s was ignored. Social workers were put in a position where they had to demand that the young person report frequently to them or engage in some sort of reparation or community service work. If they did not adhere to the order, they were quickly returned to court and custody could well have followed. The compensatory aspects of supervision found in the 'old' intermediate treatment or even in some specified activities schemes virtually disappeared (Rogowski, 1995). Importantly, the autonomy and discretion of social workers was reduced as managers asserted their control.

Anti-oppressive practice

Anti-oppressive practice, which can be linked to a radical/critical practice, developed in response to critiques of traditional social work with the aim of addressing social justice issues and empowering those receiving services (Dominelli, 2002a, 2009b). Initially, anti-discriminatory perspectives arose largely as a result of developments in relation to 'race' and gender, but they were also influenced by work in relation to lesbian and gay rights, disability and aging. It is 'race' and gender that I comment on here, as I have found them of particular relevance to my practice.

Payne (2005b), drawing on others such as Ely and Denney (1987) and Dominelli (1997), notes five perspectives in relation to race, each having implications for practice. First, assimilation assumes that migrants or minorities will assimilate to the majority culture and lifestyle, with any personal difficulties interpreted pathologically as, for instance, failures in acculturation or incorporation. Second, liberal pluralism sees all groups coexisting, with equal opportunities being assured by the law and resulting practice focusing on equal access to services. Third, cultural pluralism refers to all groups coexisting and maintaining their cultural traditions, with cultural sensitivity being essential to practice. Fourth, the structuralist perspective sees capitalist or free market societies affecting groups within them differently, with ethnic as well as class division recognised as the basis for economic and social domination of particular groups by the ruling class; practice involves, for example, confronting racism and working in alliance with black communities. Finally, the black perspective sees black and minority groups developing particular views on societies because of their history and experience, and practice includes helping black communities participate in service and practice development. The

—

structuralist and black perspectives are of particular relevance as far as radical/critical practice is concerned.

There are various feminisms as we saw in Chapter One, but what becomes most clear is that gender is the basis of important life experiences for women. A women-centred practice involves valuing women, ensuring opportunities for them to get away from caring roles or dependency on men, and avoiding conventional assumptions that women's 'ordinary' behaviour (such as offending) is particularly bad. It also questions the view that when men are involved in child abuse, the woman is in effect blamed for 'failing to protect' her children. The socialist view of feminist social work involves conscientisation and critical reflection, a dialogue between equals concerned with understanding dehumanising social structures and changing social conditions (Hanmer and Statham, (1999 [1988]). This sits well with Dominelli's (2002b) structural view of feminist theory and practice and hence radical/critical social work.

During the 1990s, approaches developed that included all forms of oppression, as well as those relating to race and gender. For example, Dalrymple and Burke (1995) followed the radical critique of the failings of traditional social work and argue for working in partnership with users, using empowerment and advocacy to make links between people's personal positions and structural inequalities. Empowerment seeks to help people gain power over decision making and action in their own lives (see, for example, Adams, 1996), while advocacy seeks to represent the interests of the powerless to powerful individuals and social structures. Mullender and Ward (1991) provide a useful, self-directed, group work approach to empowerment based on people's problems reflecting issues of oppression, policy, economy and power. Advocacy itself includes acting and arguing for peoples' interests in the field of welfare rights and in the 1980s and 1990s it became a process of increasing the capacity of people with mental health problems and disabilities to manage their own lives by defining their own needs and having a say in decision making (for example, Beresford and Croft, 1993).

A key point about anti-oppressive practice is that it tries to understand and tackle the structural causes of social problems and address their consequences by changing social relations at all possible levels (Dominelli, 2009b). As such, it was and remains a major theoretical and practice approach that responds to the needs of oppressed people who object to the failure of state services to meet needs as defined by them. Its power can by gauged by the fact there was a political 'backlash' in response to 'politically correct' approaches during the 1990s. This included changes having to be made to the Central Council for Education and Training in Social Work's Paper 30 (CCETSW, 1989), which had referred to 'endemic racism in Britain' (see Chapter Five)[1].

Despite the profound changes inflicted on Britain during Thatcher's era, it took some time to affect day-to-day social work practice, while significant developments were also able to take place in the theoretical sphere. But affect practice Thatcherism eventually did.

From child welfare to child protection

From the 1960s and into the 1970s, child abuse was essentially seen as a medico-social problem, with the emphasis on diagnosing, curing and preventing the 'disease' or syndrome. Doctors and social workers were the ones who had the skills to prevent and cure the problem. Research focused on identifying the traits of the 'abusing family', with the practitioner being expected to identify these characteristics and act accordingly. As a result of the Maria Colwell inquiry (Secretary of State for Social Services, 1974), case conferences and registers were established, with the involvement of doctors, health visitors and social workers considered crucial and the social services department, the statutory childcare agency, being pivotal. It was only in 1976 that the police's role was considered vital as up until then the medico-scientific model had remained dominant (Otway, 1996). This was to gradually change to a socio-legal model, with the emphasis on investigating, assessing and examining the evidence (Parton, 1985).

Criticisms of welfarism grew during the 1970s and deepened in the 1980s, thereby undermining the welfare consensus in childcare. In part it grew because of the neoliberal view that wherever possible people should be responsible for themselves and left to their own devices with the state only intervening as a last resort. In addition, there were concerns about poor childcare practice, the inability

—

to exploit the emphasis on prevention, and the nature and extent of interventions in people's lives in the name of welfare. Feminists brought to the fore the issue of domestic violence and its effect on women and children, thus disputing the view of the family as a safe haven, and this influenced the children's rights movement. In the 1980s, Parents Against Injustice voiced concerns about the intrusive intervention into families' lives by many social workers, these being particularly pertinent following the events in Cleveland, Rochdale and Orkney when many children were removed from their families as a result of child abuse concerns. Various child abuse inquiries also pointed to deficiencies in policy, practice, knowledge and skills and the way systems performed and interrelated. Social workers were often seen as too gullible and trusting of parents, consequently failing to intervene to protect children, or, as in the Cleveland case, as over-zealous and not respecting the rights of parents (Secretary of State for Social Services, 1988). Both the legal framework and social work practice were criticised and there were calls for a new balance between 'family autonomy and state intervention but also getting the correct balance between the power, discretion and responsibilities of the judicial, social and medical experts and agencies' (Otway, 1996, p 158).

Eventually, as a result of overwhelming criticism of the processes that sought to transform 'dysfunctional' families into 'healthy' ones, the focus was to change from working therapeutically to protecting children. Furthermore, the language used in this process changed, with terms such as 'investigation', 'assessment', dangerousness' and 'forensic evidence' now more reminiscent of law enforcement than a caring profession. As Howe (1992) put it, social workers become investigators, managers become designers of surveillance systems rather than consultants, and parents become objects of enquiry; the move is essentially from one of therapy and welfare to one of surveillance and control. Lawyers and the courts then become crucial, scrutinising social work practice and in so doing changing attitudes and the course of practice itself. Such a scenario is a way of addressing a key problem for the neoliberal state: formulating a legal basis that enables authority to intervene in family life in order to protect children but prevents all families from becoming clients of the state, while simultaneously presenting the legislation as applicable to all. The result was the 1989 Children Act.

The 1989 Act and resulting guidance and regulations sought an approach to childcare that was preventative and partnership oriented, supported families, and worked with children in need. Despite this, anxieties about child protection dominated and the notion of 'significant harm' became the criteria for state intervention via care proceedings, these in turn being the subject of legal oversight. Health and social work experts were seen as being unable to be left to make decisions alone, so under *Working Together* (Home Office et al, 1991) law and order agencies became involved in ways that they had not been previously. For social workers, an important aspect of all this was comprehensive assessment, which was an attempt to improve and clarify the social assessment of 'risk' (DH, 1988). It was hoped that the rationalisation of interagency working and procedures would be matched by developing practice skills in the assessment of individual cases. Importantly, the roles of social workers and the police were merged from the initial strategy meetings held to discuss both childcare and law enforcement issues and thereafter throughout the whole investigation process. These developments were reinforced by the *Memorandum of Good Practice* (Home Office/DH, 1992), whereby protecting children was combined with the processes of prosecuting offenders, especially in terms of gaining evidence that would stand up in a criminal court. Since then, the social work–police relationship has been, and remains, central in child protection work. This is despite the fact that critics refer to the dangers of social workers losing their identity and professionalism; dominated by the police, the argument goes, they become more focused on gaining evidence for prosecution and less concerned with providing support for the child and family. Some have even referred to the 'voluntary liquidation of a social work identity' (Garrett, 2003, p 61), this being particularly pertinent when one considers that some social work managers recently advocated social workers being trained in police questioning and interrogating techniques[2].

Despite some of the intentions of the 1989 Act, the reality of most social work with children and families throughout the 1990s until the present time has been largely one of a crisis-oriented, reactive

—

service in relation to child protection. This involves an authoritarian and controlling attitude towards families and often alienates them in the process. This was recognised by the Department of Health (DH, 1995), which argued for a refocusing on a more preventative, family support role. This may sound all well and good, but coming from a right-wing Conservative government it may have had more to do with reducing the cost of expensive child protection investigations and resulting care proceedings. In any case, unlike the aforementioned government publications, it did not have a large impact on practice.

From social work to care management with older people

Social work with older people changed significantly under Thatcherism. The move to neoliberalism meant a change from the certainties of the postwar era when policy and practice consisted largely of the state providing financial provision and care services, thereby delivering security to people living into later life, with social workers being the key actors in this service-oriented approach (Philips, 1996). However, the promise of a cradle-to-grave welfare state gave way to the insecurities of a marketplace where those with financial resources had greater access to welfare provision and the majority had to cope with increased isolation and insecurity. Policy changes introduced by the 1990 National Health Service and Community Care Act were supposed to promote 'choice' by empowering 'consumers'. For social work practice, this again necessitated a move from an emphasis on the therapeutic relationship, or at least a relationship of some kind, to one of assessment of individual need and care management.

The 1990 Act raised the profile of 'community care', which in essence refers to more cost-effective care, with the overriding objective being to make as many people as possible self-reliant. The White Paper *Caring for People* (DH, 1989) sought to enable people to live as normal a life as possible, facilitate independence and empower individuals with regard to lifestyle and service choices. This included increasing state expenditure on private care for older people, with local authorities acting as enablers rather than direct providers, the rationale being to provide wider choice. This concerted effort to shift provision to the private sector also entailed a commodification of social relationships between the formal and informal sectors, with purchasing and contracting arrangements creating an illusion of securing care provision. The reality for the majority of older people was that genuine choice was lacking and increasingly the only option was to rely on family carers, usually women. Such older people may well have remained in the community, but not necessarily in circumstances of their own choosing.

The contracting arrangements meant that accountability was achieved through increased monitoring, regulation and inspection of the quality of care and standards of practice. This can be a positive thing, but can also mean increased uncertainty for both those providing the services and those on the receiving end. Regulation also allowed the state to retreat, selling off its residential care provision and allowing the private sector to provide services within the context of registration and inspection. What remains for the state – the provision of services proportionate to perceived risk and attempts to deal with uncertainty by administrative (and now managerial) definition (Bamford, 1990) – is controlled by managers, with practitioner autonomy minimised by increased rules, routines and procedures, even though this means risk aversion often takes precedence over flexibility and responsiveness to needs. Taken as a whole, this can be seen as transforming the nature of social services from a welfare agency run by professionals to a customer-centred group of facilities run by managers (Langan and Clarke, 1994).

These changes had a negative impact on social work practice, with so-called *needs*-led assessment and care management being central to the reforms. The notion of meeting needs might have been the stated objective for the changes, but too often social workers became engaged in financial rationalisations, more concerned about the need for value for money than effective care packages. Admittedly, the change in terminology from client to user can be viewed positively, reflecting a change in the balance of power between professionals and older people. But separating the assessment from service provision reinforces the view that social work with older people is about providing services that can be seen simply as a technical operation carried out by filling in forms in a standardised format.

—

The real danger is that the forms become ends in themselves, with an administrative or managerial rather than person-centred model of practice coming to dominate. The focus is on gate-keeping access to resources and case coordination rather than engaging in a therapeutic relationship.

The probation service: from social work to control and punishment

Another service that was to feel the brunt of Thatcherism was probation, which underwent a transformation in the late 1960s and early 1970s. Prior to this, it was marginal to criminal justice, social work and central and local government, although it did impose control on its charges by its very existence as the antechamber to less pleasant forms of punishment, namely custody (Harris, 1996). This marginality changed as the service was moved to centre-stage by governments anxious to impose order and reason throughout the social world. Like other public services, policy was to be centralised, but administrative and managerial responsibility for delivering it was devolved, tight financial controls and accountability were imposed, and competition, emphasising efficiency and effectiveness, was injected from the mixed economy (Home Office, 1987). These changes meant that instead of being a relatively small agency responsible for doing good at the fringes of the criminal justice system, it became a large, complex organisation responsible for delivering non-custodial and post-custodial community corrections (or, as they are now called, punishments). During the 1970s, successive governments began this process, appreciating the central role probation could play in penal policy. For instance, following the 1972 Criminal Justice Act community service and day-centre places were introduced, hostel places were increased and suspended sentence supervision orders became a new responsibility. Following the 1979 Thatcher victory, successive governments increasingly sought to define the service as an arm of the criminal justice and penal systems complementary to the police and prison services. The aim was to move away from probation as a social work service operating in the criminal justice system or even as a criminal justice agency working to an explicit social work base (Aldridge and Eadie, 1997). A key document was on

—

objectives and priorities (Home Office, 1984). This led to the cash limiting of budgets, performance-related pay, an obligation to commit 5% of budget to voluntary organisations, the transformation of the probation order as a sentence in its own right, the introduction of national standards and competencies, and, significantly, the location of training strategy in the Home Office Training Unit.

By the 1990s, probation saw 'an increasing rift with government, the exposure by quantitative measurement of the limitations of its efficiency and effectiveness, ever increasing pressure on the service to define itself as the government [wished it to be] defined, and a failure on the service's part to agree activities with which it is happy, which it can deliver and which will carry support among the informed public' (Harris, 1996, p 129). This ended up with the service coming under political attack following the appointment of Michael Howard as Home Secretary in 1993 (McIvor and Raynor, 2007). He famously announced that 'prison works', while probation was seen as a 'soft' option that saw offenders as victims of society who should be helped rather than punished. In 1995, the Home Office proposed the abolition of the requirement that probation officers hold the Diploma in Social Work (DipSW) or its earlier equivalents (Home Office, 1995). Following an orchestrated press campaign (see Aldridge and Eadie, 1997), during which for a period there was no training at all, the link between probation and social work training was broken. Under New Labour, probation was to be moved ever closer to the prison service with both coming together to form the National Offender Management Service. The situation can be characterised by seeing probation, at the behest of government, increasingly working with offenders in a 'law and order' controlling and authoritarian way, and with officers increasingly subservient to managerial decision making and control by the imposition of increased bureaucracy and proceduralisation. As we have seen, all this was similar to what happened with social work with young offenders.

Conclusion

Margaret Thatcher's and John Major's premiership saw the embracing of neoliberalism but for a time social work could still develop in progressive, even radical/critical ways. However, the right wing of the Conservative Party had always wanted to sanitise social work and to remove any oppositional or ideological infection (Garrett, 2003). Social work's value base and awareness of factors relating to class, 'race', gender and other forms of oppression was a concern, and social work was also becoming tainted because of its association with the public sector and the postwar settlement between capital and labour via the trade union movement. It is not surprising that social work and the agencies in which it operated were to be reconstructed, since this was consistent with the central themes characterising the reconstruction of welfare and the welfare state more generally (Parton, 1996b).

This refiguring of social work had a number of features. First, there was an emphasis on market principles, often referred to as the 'quasi-market' (Le Grand and Bartlett, 1993), including a split between purchasing and providing responsibilities, a concern for services to be based on need and the assessment of risk rather than historic demand and service levels, the delegation of authority for budgetary control and the pursuit of choice through provider competition. Second, there was the introduction of contractual rather than hierarchical accountability whereby relationships within and between welfare organisations were specific and formally described and costed. Third, there was an attempt to develop more responsive organisations where responsibilities and decisions were devolved and the user/consumer more directly involved. This all went hand in hand with the prioritisation of various performance indicators, outcome measures and business plans along with increased proceduralisation.

Such developments led to more fluid and fragmented arrangements whereby social work and social services were also provided by the voluntary and private sectors (see Carter, 1998). Staff other than social workers were increasingly seen as more appropriate in the actual provision of many services, and the role and practices of managers were key as they supplanted the activities of social workers and the forms of knowledge they drew on. Such changes were to continue and intensify under New Labour as social work was subjected to further challenges.

—

Notes

[1] This is despite those (for example, McLaughlin, 2008) who argue that the 'backlash' was exaggerated and that its critique has become incorporated into mainstream political and organisational discourses.

[2] During May 2009, letters appeared in the journal *Community Care* arguing for social workers to incorporate police models of investigation, planning and questioning so as to gather information about perpetrators. There was also a call for social workers to attend police-run interviewing skills workshops (Lowman, 2009).

FOUR

New Labour: new challenges and (fewer) opportunities

> From the position of acceptance to globalisation as an uncontrollable phenomenon ... New Labour consolidated the Conservatives' reforms and pushed beyond them, ensuring that public services, such as social work, were drawn deeper into managerial, market-orientated ways of thinking and practising. As in many other countries, what began as a national project under neo-conservative governments became generalised as part of the economic agenda of globalisation. (Harris and White, 2009a, p 3)

The landslide general election victory of Tony Blair in 1997 saw John Major's government, with its reputation of sleaze and corruption, ousted. After many years in opposition, the 'old' social democratic, to some even socialist, Labour Party had been rebranded by Blair, Gordon Brown and others as New Labour. They had argued that any suggestion of socialism was unlikely to appeal to the new middle classes, so a new direction for the party was needed. Despite the electorate's calls for change, there was no major transformation in terms of political ideology, economic and social policy.

Although New Labour espoused the Third Way, when the party came to power it continued with the neoliberal offensive of the Thatcher and Major governments. Its 1997 general election manifesto stated that policies could not be based on those of 1947 or 1967 (Labour Party, 1997) and, as with Thatcher, there was a repudiation of the social democratic compact. Blair and his guru Giddens (for example, 1994, 1998) argued for the Third Way, which did not conform to the 'old' left or right wing of politics. In essence, however, New Labour's 'new' ideology involved the embracement of free

—

market globalisation, with flexible labour markets and flexible workers being the order of the day with the aim of producing a competitive economy that relied on a competitive society in the global economy (Mooney and Law, 2007). While the social democratic era was based on the corporatism of government, labour and business making and implementing policy, under the neoliberalism of New Labour, government largely operated at the behest of multinational corporations; witness the oft-repeated reference to the need for 'light' or 'soft' touch regulation so as not to stifle competitiveness and profitability.

It is within notions of the competitive economy and society that the drive for national renewal comes to the fore, and, as far as public services and the welfare state are concerned, it encompasses the mantras of 'reform' and 'modernisation'. The Third Way saw welfare reform and modernisation as crucial, including widespread attacks on 'welfare dependency' and the reform of the public services, again including attacks on what was constructed as the 'producer interests' in the public sector (Ferguson et al, 2002). This agenda soon affected personal social services, leading to the demise of social services departments, and seriously impinged on social work itself.

This chapter begins with a discussion of Third Way ideology, particularly as it relates to welfare. Subsequently, I turn to what happened to social work over the New Labour years. This includes regulation, inspection and organisational changes and the 'reform' and 'modernisation' of social work with children and families. Privatisation possibilities and the authoritarian response to 'problem families' are also covered. I then consider changes in relation to social work with young offenders as well as with adults and older people.

New Labour, the Third Way and the welfare state

Although it is rarely acknowledged, New Labour's ideology drew on much of that of the New Right. Even though Giddens (for example, 1994, 1998, 2000, 2001) provided the intellectual background, and preferred the term the 'Third Way', it is best described as the neoliberal way. Giddens could see no alternatives to capitalism and contended all that can be done is to determine how and in what ways it can be governed and regulated. There is an acceptance of the free market and a belief that individuals should take on more responsibility for their lives, including their own welfare.

The beginnings of New Labour's approach to welfare can be found in the report of the Commission on Social Justice (1994), which was set up by the late Labour leader John Smith (see, for example, Powell, 1999, 2000). The report set out three approaches to economic and social policy. The old left was seen as being concerned with the distribution of wealth rather than its creation, with social justice achieved primarily through the benefits system. The New Right saw social justice being achieved through reducing public services and freeing the markets, even though this would lead to extremes of affluence and poverty. For the Commission, the preferred alternative was the Middle Way, which was then to equate with Giddens' Third Way of 'investment in human capital ... rather than the direct provision of economic maintenance. In place of the welfare state we should put the social investment state, operating in the context of a positive welfare society' (1998, p 117). Social justice and economic efficiency are seen as two sides of the same coin, both being 'good for business', this coincided with the New Labour emphasis on education and welfare to work helped by an active, preventative welfare state, rather than simply a passive one that pays benefits. Redistribution, through the tax and benefit system, and thus steps towards genuine equality, are rejected. To the extent that redistribution is addressed, it relates to redistributing opportunities through education, training and paid employment, which results in equality of outcome becoming redefined to equality of opportunity. The focus is on inclusion and exclusion rather than equality per se, with paid work and education being the mechanisms of inclusion. This means ensuring that everyone is given the opportunity to maximise their productive contribution to the formal economy, which amounts to developing their full potential in terms of their productive, rather than their human, potential.

When it comes to citizenship, while traditionally the right stresses the duties of citizenship and the left stresses the rights of citizens, the Third Way involves a welfare state based on rights and duties. Giddens' (1998) motto is 'no rights without responsibilities', ultimately

—

resulting in a belief in conditional welfare. For instance, in relation to employment, the New Deal provided various opportunities to work that individuals, including lone parents and disabled people, have a responsibility to take up, enduring penalties if they do not. More recently, the 2008 Welfare Reform Act replaced 'passive' incapacity benefit with 'active' employment support allowance. Conditionality draws on the Clinton administrations in the US, a key criticism being that most of the responsibilities and obligations are borne by those on the bottom layers of society and not the powerful at the top.

There are two other components of the Third Way that require comment. First, there is the emphasis on combining public and private provision and increasing partnerships with civil society; it is the mixed economy of welfare. There may be a willingness to use state action, but this has to be limited and increasingly complemented by private, voluntary and informal sector provision. One has only to recall the growing involvement of the private sector in health, education and, along with the voluntary and informal sector, in social services/care. Second, social expenditure in itself is not seen as being a good thing. Instead, the aim is the more effective use of public money between and across government departments, with issues of economy and efficiency coming to the fore along with a focus on 'choice' and 'consumer rights'. Furthermore, there is 'good' and 'bad' public spending, with 'investment' in health and education considered to be 'good' and social security spending in areas such as unemployment (when people should actually be working) considered to be 'bad'. The level of spending is also no longer the yardstick of government action in the public interest; rather, it is how and what the money is spent on that counts. Treasury objectives and targets dominate, thereby ensuring that government departments keep to their plans. This extends to public services more generally and necessitates effective regulatory and inspection regimes.

The Third Way was, therefore, not particularly distinctive or new, simply because of this continuity with the New Right rather than, as one might have expected, 'old' labour. Many of its policies have simply 'out-Toried the Tories' (Powell, 2000, p 54) and if anything hark back rather than look forward. Building the welfare state around work is perhaps little more than a more humane version of the 'less eligibility'

—

concept of the New Poor Law. Added to this is the focus on moving away from traditional welfare statism, of disengaging society from the state and moving towards civil society, leading to the redrawing of the boundaries between the individual and the state. People are thereby urged to become more responsible and make provision for the risks facing themselves and their families, even though this in itself can be a risky business. Moreover, greater responsibility means more severe consequences for failure on the part of the 'irresponsible', although this makes it difficult to reconcile the link between responsibility and inclusion. In summary, although New Labour were keen to promote the idea of the responsibilised and empowered citizen, a key aspect of citizenship under New Labour was actually the abandonment of the citizen – the dismantling of the safeguards built during postwar welfare capitalism against the demands and inequities of the market (Clarke, 2005).

It can be argued that New Labour took neoliberal doctrines and policies and 'radicalised them' (Callinicos, 2001, p 121). If we take the organisational and professional reform of social work, for example, Giddens (1998) favours the market and private enterprise over the public sector because the latter is staffed by vested interest groups. Government and state agencies are also urged to 'modernise', be transparent and *customer*, rather than client or service user, oriented. Further, 'modernisation' itself is equated with ensuring that public service staff, held to be responsible for past inefficiency and rigidity, are brought into line, with those public services having profit potential being transferred to the private sector. Related to this, the type of welfare provision advocated is 'strenuous welfare', linked with conditionality, with this being provided by a range of business-focused, entrepreneurial managerial powers over welfare workers (see Mooney and Law, 2007).

Notwithstanding the Third Way rhetoric, then, 'neoliberalism' has served, often implicitly, to provide the dominant, or hegemonic, core for the 'transformation' that occurred under New Labour (Garrett, 2009b, p 140). The result is that the bequest of the New Labour governments of the 1990s and 2000s was similar to that of previous New Right governments: 'increased capital accumulation and privatisation alongside growing inequality of income and opportunity,

—

social marginalisation and moral authoritarianism' (Ferguson and Woodward, 2009, p 44). As far as moral authoritarianism is concerned, an example includes the incarceration of parents of children who irregularly attend school despite the damaging effects this can have on families. Another example, and one that particularly relates to social work, was New Labour's policies towards failed asylum seekers. These included restricting their social and welfare rights so that they are not incentivised to stay and are encouraged to return home. Social workers are often drawn into this process by having to inform the Home Office about such people, thereby being forced into a coercive and authoritarian role even to the extent of taking children into care if their parents cannot provide reasonable care for them (Humphries, 2004; Fell and Hayes, 2007).

As mentioned above, New Labour policies affected social work in a number of important ways. There was the emergence of new structures for its regulation and inspection, organisational changes, the beginnings of new 'professions', increasing direction from the centre, a fixation with targets and performance indicators, and an emphasis on the 'modern' and the advantages of information and communication technology. All this coincided with increasing moves towards privatisation of services and the gradual criminalisation of child welfare discourses, for example, the moral panic about the antisocial behaviour of young people and families (Garrett, 2003).

New Labour, new regulation, new organisations and the sidelining of social work

Four years after the election of Tony Blair, Bill Jordan noted that 'social work in the UK seems to be fairing worse under a Labour government than it did under eighteen years of Conservative administrations' (Jordan, 2001, p 527). One has only to recall the way social work was restricted in the new areas created for engaging with deprived children and families, including Sure Start and the Children's Fund, which were set up outside local authority social services departments. Social work was also largely absent in the policies and practices promoting social exclusion. Some nine years later, Jordan's words still ring true, with the very words 'social work'

—

rarely mentioned positively. Related to this are two important New Labour changes which focused on the regulation and inspection of social work (covered further in Chapter Six in relation to the social work business) together with the organisational frameworks within which social work and social care are delivered. These developments have all contributed to an element of airbrushing the very words 'social work' out of existence.

The 2000 Care Standards Act introduced changes that came into effect in 2001 and three of these are of particular relevance to social work. First, the Central Council for the Education and Training in *Social Work* was replaced by the General Social *Care* Council, with similar bodies being established in the rest of the UK. Its aim is to regulate social work training and the social work and care workforce in England. Second, the Social *Care* Institute for Excellence (SCIE) was established to identify and disseminate evidence-based practice, with the demise of the National Institute of *Social Work* subsequently occurring in 2003. Third, the National *Care* Standards Commission was introduced to regulate adult social care, undergoing several transformations before becoming the *Care* Quality Commission. The obvious question is why the use of the word 'care' and the absence of 'social work' in all these name changes? It shows the disdain with which New Labour has held social work as a profession as well as the continued desire to cleanse and remove any oppositional possibilities to the neoliberal project.

As for inspection, arguably the most important point to note is the increasing influence of Ofsted especially after the demise of social services departments and the introduction of children's trusts. Ofsted was originally established to inspect education but increasingly took over aspects of social services culminating in the scrutiny of children's services, the current combination of education and children's social care. A key criticism is that the organisation lacks the knowledge and understanding needed to inspect social work, this being one of the factors acknowledged in relation to the Baby Peter case.

As for organisational changes, New Labour was responsible for the creation of new agencies, including statutorily enforced partnerships and quangos. This is partly a result of an emphasis on changed patterns of interprofessional working highlighted in various government

—

publications arguing for the integration of health and social care (Lymbery, 2004a). Such tendencies initially largely concerned adults but similar changes emerged in relation to children, young people and families.

An early example of such organisational change, together with the New Labour emphasis on interprofessional working, was the creation of youth offending teams (YOTs) following the implementation of the 1998 Crime and Disorder Act (see below). In a different vein, the Connexions Service, providing personal advisers for all 13- to 19-year-olds, began to be phased in during 2001. The focus was on the education, training and work needs of young people, and there was a general concern with problems faced by, or perhaps more appropriately, posed by young people (Garrett, 2003). It is not hard to see that the service had the potential to overlap and encroach on social work. Similar comments apply to the emergence of various care, support and adviser 'professionals', all of which can be viewed as a renewed attempt at the governing or 'policing of families' (Donzelot, 1979). The important point is that, as in other areas of the public services, work that was once the preserve of highly trained professionals is increasingly being carried out by less qualified staff. This has not resulted in less pressure on overworked professionals, but in cut-price services for the public Social workers, for instance, are generally not being freed up to concentrate on complex cases, with much of their time increasingly spent on inputting data instead so as to meet targets and performance indicators. In fact, perhaps the easiest way to discern New Labour's disregard for social work is to note Blair's major speech about public services made in Newcastle in January 2002. He referred to teachers, the police, nurses, doctors and hospital staff more generally but, significantly, not social workers (Garrett, 2009b, p 69).

The most significant organisational changes occurred after the Victoria Climbié Inquiry (Laming, 2003) into the death of a young girl as a result of injuries inflicted by her carers. The apparent inability of agencies to work together highlighted and the government subsequently published *Every Child Matters* (DfES, 2004). This in turn led to the 2004 Children Act, which aimed to transform children's services and ensure that every child had the support they needed to be healthy, stay safe, enjoy and achieve, make a positive contribution and achieve economic well-being. The Act sought to enhance the integration of health, education, social services/care and other services, thereby encouraging professionals to avoid working and thinking within a bunker-like mentality as they had done previously from within their 'own' departments. The latter were seen by New Labour as having separate cultures, values and management styles, which meant they had difficulty working together (Pierson, 2010). Actually there was limited evidence of the need or reason for services to be changed (Frost, 2005)[1], but nevertheless the departments' 'silos' were dismantled and replaced with the supposedly more integrated services in the form of children's trusts. This led to the demise of social services in 2006, meaning in essence that local government no longer provided a safe, supportive environment for the practice of social work.

Under New Labour, therefore, social work underwent various changes at the regulation, inspection and organisational levels, but what differences occurred as far as practice was concerned?

New Labour and social work with children and families

At the outset, it has to be acknowledged that there were some positive developments in relation to social work with children and families during New Labour's period in office. One example, influenced by feminist insights, is the recognition that domestic violence can have a negative impact on children and that practice has to address this (see Hughes and Owen, 2009). On the other hand, social work 'remains shadowy, portrayed either as anxious monitoring or decisive protection, or even tough enforcement, but never as sensitive, aware, dialogical and flexible negotiation' (Jordan with Jordan, 2000, p 125). This description still rings true, with the negative connotations continuing to dominate. And when one considers the detail of practice, it becomes clear that the changes that have occurred amount to the increased bureaucratisation and control of the social work task. An example of the latter is the introduction of separate duty/initial assessment and long-term teams, and the separation of after-care teams for looked after children from children and families teams.

—

Both contribute to the increasing fragmentation of the social work task, which amounts to deskilling[2].

Of key importance, however, has been the introduction of looked after children (LAC) materials, the Framework for Assessment and the 'electronic turn' (Garrett, 2003, 2005), all of which occur within a managerial ethos. These developments are now the hallmarks of practice with children and families, although it should be noted that the LAC materials were actually introduced during the mid-1990s under John Major in an effort to improve the outcomes for LAC. This began a process that, under New Labour, was to see a proliferation of centrally devised assessment schedules and other paper and electronic 'tools' for the use of social workers and other 'professionals' working with children and families. Two other important issues to consider are the introduction of social work practices for LAC, and new ways of dealing with the re-emergence of the phenomenon of 'problem families' (see Garrett, 2009b).

The obsession with paper and electronic tools

The LAC materials involve numerous forms, and one only needs a glance to be quickly struck by the amount of repetition and duplication involved, as well as various other problems. Although some social workers have found ways of using the forms positively (see Charles and Wilton, 2004), more often completing them is a time-consuming, repetitive task that takes social workers away from what they should be doing, namely building relationships with children and families, and working with them on issues as defined by them. Another concern is that when it comes to parenting, the LAC system simply does not take into account one of the main reasons *why* children become accommodated in the first place, namely poverty. Perhaps the forms say more about the middle-class concerns of the academics that devised them. Then there is the fact that many of the forms are in checklist format, with intrusive questions on issues such as drug use and sexuality, which means that young people are often treated as objects rather than human beings. Finally, as Garrett (2003, pp 36-7) argues, perhaps the LAC forms are really more about two overriding narratives: first, ensuring that young people are adequately prepared for the 'world of work' and that they are compliant, well-presented employees who are able to function in 'flexible' markets; and second, focusing on the need to ensure that the 'crimo-genic' proclivities of the children of the unemployed and poor are detected, regulated and contained.

Although the LAC forms can make empathetic and non-directive engagement and interaction with children and young people difficult, it is the association between these forms and managerialism that I want to emphasise here. This is apparent in the notion of 'outcomes' evident in many of the forms, involving a concern with the measuring of inputs, processes and outputs. There is an implicit impatience with the uncertainties and ambiguities of social work and, again drawing on the Clinton administrations in the US, there is a concern with the way welfare systems must 'work', promote social order and not hinder the process of capital accumulation. It is linked to the operation of the market in welfare services, whereby crude outcome data, available from LAC forms as well as other sources, helps in drawing up contractual specifications in relation to, for example, children placed in private residential care or with foster carers working for private fostering agencies. Put bluntly, the more difficulties or problems the child or young person has, the more these private companies can charge for caring for them.

But it was the introduction of the standardised assessment framework that was central to the changes affecting social work with children and families under New Labour (DH et al, 2000). This superseded the 'orange book' (DH, 1988) ostensibly because the latter was followed mechanistically and used as a tick-box checklist, although this comment is surely ironic given the proliferation of questionnaires and scales in the new framework's package of materials. The stated aim was also to get away from social work focusing on child protection in a reactive, policing role; instead the new framework introduced an initial assessment for all children in need in the hope of developing an increased emphasis on family support. For more complex and/or child protection cases, in-depth core assessments were required.

A fundamental criticism of the assessment framework, as with the LAC forms, is its uncritical acceptance of current economic and social arrangements, which are presented as the unquestioned foundations of familial and dynamics and interpersonal relationships. Initially, there was some flexibility for social workers to use their own narrative to describe and explain the reality of the problems and difficulties facing children and families, but, as we shall see, this has been reduced by the 'electronic turn'. In any case, once the forms are completed, unless there are child protection concerns, little actually occurs in terms of help and support for the children and families involved. Often all they can expect is to be told their parenting is 'good enough', perhaps with some advice about, or referral to, other agencies (Rogowski, 2009). As Smith (2008, p 161) puts it, 'assessment processes ... are being utilised at least partly to justify screening out some needs, and redefining them as someone else's problem, or as insufficiently serious to warrant intervention, or sometimes as just intractable and beyond help'. In addition, again like the LAC documents, such assessments, in part at least, appear to be underpinned by the functional objective to manage risk and police people who are socially marginalised.

The framework is rooted in New Labour's modernising project and is linked to the Quality Protects initiative to improve outcomes for children in need[3]. Three systems or domains – the child's developmental needs, parenting capacity, and family and environmental factors – have to be taken into account when considering safeguarding and promoting the welfare of the child. It was hoped such considerations would help ensure that the referral and assessment process discriminated between different types and levels of need, and produce a timely service response. But surely, as with its LAC predecessor, the social work practice it promotes 'risks becoming merely a composite set of technical assessment tasks driven by 'evidence-based knowledge' about 'what works'' (Garrett, 2003, p 80).

Under New Labour, a focus on evidence-based practice has been a feature of social work, and few would disagree that practitioners require evidence to shape their interventions. However, there are also serious problems with this proposition. First, evidence-based practice is based on positivist and empirical science, and represents an extension of technical rationality into the social work field. This is surely antithetical to the essence of social work because practice takes place in problem areas that are inherently messy, confusing and not amenable to technical solutions (Smith, 2004). Order and certainty – knowing that something is single, unified, measurable, visible and, furthermore, 'works' – cannot always be realised in social work. This is because the social world is inherently unpredictable and uncertain in ways in which the natural world, at least in principle, is not. Second, what should count as evidence is problematic in the sense that it is policy makers' views that currently dominate rather than the views of social workers and users. Unlike the medical profession, so-called evidence comes from outside social work rather than from within it. A good example is the evidence from social work's 1980s involvement with young offenders, namely that diversion from the youth justice system together with genuine alternatives to custody did have an impact on youth crime. This did not sit easily with the Tories and then New Labour wanting to be tough on crime, and hence it was disregarded.

The fact that New Labour's paper, or increasingly electronic, tools have a 'narrow, normative and prescriptive view of the world and economic relationships' (Garrett, 2005, p 543) is not the only difficulty; its embracing of a positivistic view of social science that is seen to be above and beyond 'ideology' is also problematic. This is because New Labour's approach was in itself ideological, in that the framework is imbued with a preoccupation with 'new paternalism' and 'social exclusion'. The former aims to reduce poverty and other social problems by directive and supervisory means, and can be linked to the conditional welfare referred to above. The latter has the potential to mask poverty and questions of income and wealth distribution, and unproblematically sees paid work as the mechanism of social inclusion. There is no recognition that for many, work can be poorly paid, insecure and consist of dead-end jobs. Despite this, as Hall (1998, p 12) puts it, 'not since the workhouse has labour been so fervently and single-mindedly valorised'. Despite the claims by the framework's formulators (Rose and Aldgate, 2000), 'ideology' and 'ethical and professional practice' cannot be easily separated out.

The Common Assessment Framework (CAF), another New Labour 'tool', was introduced in the hope that the majority of children with additional needs could be dealt with by common

—

assessments carried out by schools, childcare providers, children's centres, health services and the voluntary sector. The aim was to improve interagency working with such children and avoid families having to repeat themselves to various agencies. But, as is often the case these days, the focus has ended up on the assessment aspect of the tool rather than on direct help for children and families. For many, CAFs are an administrative burden that does not guarantee the provision of any additional services. They simply increase the level of paperwork and consequently the time spent away from direct work with children and their families. Parents often find CAF meetings bewildering, again amounting to little more than a form-filling exercise. In addition, other professionals such as health visitors and teachers often do not see it as part of their role to complete these forms. When they contact a social worker about a child or young person's difficulties, they usually do not want to be simply told to 'fill in a CAF form'. But there are two other, more fundamental, problems with CAFs.

First, the term 'additional needs' is ill defined and could have a negative impact on how children view themselves and are viewed by others. Following Foucault, it can be argued that constant surveillance shapes the experiences of children (Foley and Rixon, 2008). Continuous monitoring and questions about their feelings, parents and experiences can actually be shaped by such formal assessment procedures along with informal daily interactions. Put simply, if they are continually asked, for example, if 'daddy frightens/ scares you', their replies could lead to child protection concerns that turn out to be groundless because 'daddy' has shouted at them and told them to stop doing something.

Second, it could be argued that the use of CAFs is hastening the demise of a social work identity. Essentially, CAFs are about what traditional, preventative social work was about (and in the past it was far more likely that actual services would be provided to meet needs). But if others, such as health visitors and teachers, are to take on this role, what remains for social work with children and families? At best it would only leave child protection cases. But if this were the scenario, would there be a need for so many social workers, or even social work itself, as arguably the police could deal with such situations? We should step back and question much of what comes from, and is then enforced by, the 'powers that be'. Like changes in relation to other professions, attempts to move things forward should emanate from, or at least include, the views of social workers themselves, rather than be imposed from above.

The 'electronic turn' was another key theme of social work with children and families under New Labour (Garrett, 2005). Influenced by developments in the private sector, information and communication technologies (ICTs) are increasingly fulfilling a crucial role in terms of technologising and marketising the public sector (Harris, 2003). The need for efficiency and more effective targeting, as well as ensuring that the requirements of 'consumers' dominate those of service providers, are the familiar arguments supporting the increasing reliance on the new technology. But, as noted in Chapter One, what has happened with the Integrated Children's System (ICS) shows how disastrous the unthinking introduction of ICTs can be, with social workers now having to spend most of their time simply inputting data (Hall et al, 2008). For example, electronic core assessments consist of over 50 pages of tick-box answers and unsurprisingly are not child or family friendly, nor are they acceptable for case conferences or court. Even when compared with the 'old' initial and core assessments, they leave much to be desired. One of the main reasons for this is that they allow little scope for social workers to express their own view of a situation, relying instead on what the computer and in turn their relevant agency and the government wants. It is not surprising that the Social Work Task Force established in response to the Baby Peter case had problems with ICS at the top of its agenda. A key question to address is whether it assists in meeting the needs of children and families. Another is how social workers can be expected to protect/ safeguard children when in effect they are prevented from spending any significant time with them or their families simply because they have to devote most of their time to the computer.

—

Practising privatisation

'Pilot' proposals to privatise social work services for looked after children are another concern (see Garrett, 2009b). As was the case during John Major's prime ministership, the plight of looked after children was the focus of attention for New Labour governments, including concerns with educational performance and seeing adoption as a solution to problems in the care system (for example, Garrett, 2002). In 2007, a White Paper (DfES, 2007) appeared, drawing on the report of a working group led by Le Grand (2007) recommending the introduction of social work practices for looked after children, with various pilots subsequently being established. They entailed small groups of social workers working with such children and young people and they were commissioned by, but independent of, local authorities.

Le Grand (2007) rightly argues that social workers are frustrated by the procedures, bureaucracy and managerialism, including the 'electronic turn', that take them away from direct work with service users. He also comments on social workers' strong moral purpose, idealism and commitment to rectifying injustice when they first enter the profession. However, he goes on, once in the job, they are often deprived of autonomy and overwhelmed by form filling and meaningless targets. So far so good, but this situation is then 'blamed' on local authorities, notwithstanding that it was a New Labour government that inflicted this private sector managerialism on them in the first place. Unfortunately, the working group fails to acknowledge this. Instead, in order to address the problems, practices are seen as providing an opportunity for social workers and in turn 'their' children, giving the former the autonomy and freedom from a complex management structure to put the child above everything else. Professional decision making, the argument continues, replaces decisions by managers, and, further, social workers will have a personal financial stake in all of this.

Looking past the New Labour spin, the situation is a lot more complex. The high moral tone of Le Grand and his colleagues is less than sincere. While the frustrations of social workers to which they refer are real and significant, there is no acknowledgement that they have been caused by the neoliberal context in which they have to operate. They simply cannot be solved by inflicting even more neoliberalism, with its belief in the market and the private sector, on to social work. The obvious charge is that social work practices mean local authority children's services for looked after children are to be privatised and that such children are to be commodified. Le Grand and his colleagues even concede that such practices could eventually take over child protection/safeguarding and services for children in need, which is certainly a worrying scenario.

The re-emergence of 'problem families'[4]

When it comes to the renewed discourse on 'problem families' and the subsequent 'sin-bin' solution proposed for them, the Respect Task Force's (2006) action plan was of particular significance. For New Labour, such families were the opposite of 'hardworking families' and are perceived as belonging to another age – 'families that are unable or unwilling to exhibit a commitment to be self-activating and responsibilized neo-liberal citizens' (Garrett, 2009b, p 101). Dealing with them was a central focus in the drive against antisocial behaviour, and following the action plan this included 'intensive family support projects' comprising outreach services, often with a residential component. They became mandatory and were to be 'rolled out' to all local authorities having initially appeared in Dundee and then in six towns and cities in the north of England. When it comes to the research into the pilots (see Garrett, 2009b, pp 106-16), various points can be noted. First, many if not most of the families involved had characteristics of poverty and ill health. Second, their involvement was based on a combination of persuasion and coercion, with compliance often being forthcoming simply because of the lack of alternative housing options. In addition, it could be argued that those families who cooperated and spoke favourably of their experience might simply have been the most compliant or least able to resist coercion. Third, notions of control and intrusion, resulting in the infantilisation of the adults, were apparent. Finally, some of the researchers 'appear far too ... emphatic when, despite an apparent lack of sufficient and convincing supporting data, they maintain that the projects which they examined offer a "lifeline" to families' (Garrett,

—

2009b, pp 115). Overall, perhaps the researchers could 'have been a little bolder in critically interpreting their, often complex, findings which reveal a good deal about the trajectory of the fragmenting, and increasingly authoritarian, outer edges of the neo-liberal "welfare" state' (Garrett, 2009b, p 115).

One could even argue that the residential component of these projects is a form of 'pre-emptive or preventative detention' (Rose, 2000, p 330). They are perhaps examples of neoliberal punitiveness in relation to people facing problems and difficulties, others being residential provision for teenage parents or asylum seekers. They may also indicate the general direction of intervention with children and families, including that provided by social workers, in the future. They provide further evidence of the neoliberal project's incursion into the social domain, and bearing in mind the involvement of Action for Children in such projects, they may well contain an implicit element of privatisation.

The changes to social work and other interventions with children and families outlined here have taken place as managerialism retains, and even increases, its hold over the social work task. The major concern of the managerial ethos is to meet targets and performance indicators, with social work supervision largely consisting of questions about whether computer exemplar assessments have been completed within the allotted timescale. There is little, if any, concern about the quality of such assessments, but merely a requirement that they have been done and that there are 'no empty boxes'. At times one wonders if they are ever even read. So it is with LAC forms. The rise and now increased dominance of managerialism is covered further in Chapter Six, so at this stage let us turn to social work with young offenders.

New Labour, new punitiveness: social work with young offenders

As noted earlier, social work success with young offenders during the 1980s was ignored as the 'populist punitiveness' discourse came to dominate (Bottoms, 1995). The election of a New Labour government led some to believe that there would be more progressive policies in relation to youth crime and that, to quote Tony Blair, the 'causes of crime' would be seriously addressed. Sadly, they were to be disappointed because Blair was to concentrate on the first half of the now famous phrase 'tough on crime, tough on the causes of crime', as evidenced by New Labour's flagship 1998 Crime and Disorder Act (see, for example, Goldson, 1999, 2000). Key provisions included the replacement of cautions with reprimands and final warnings, the possibility of children under ten being made the subject of local curfews, and parents of convicted young people being made the subject of parenting orders. There was also an increased focus on incarceration, with detention and training orders replacing secure training orders and sentences in young offender's institutions for young people aged 12-17 years. Finally, an array of other orders were introduced, including referral orders, reparation orders, drug treatment and testing orders and action plan orders, these all being in addition to those orders grounded in the 1991 Criminal Justice Act.

New Labour also widened the concept of popular punitiveness through its concern with antisocial behaviour and an expectation on young people to show respect. This 'criminalising of nuisance' resulted in the introduction of antisocial behaviour orders, which have been criticised on the grounds of being unfair, unjust, disproportionate, stigmatising, criminalising and, not least, ineffective (Squires, 2008; Millie, 2009).

New Labour's 'get tough' approach to youth crime is carried out by YOTs comprising representatives from the police, probation, social work, education and health services. The focus is on swift administration of justice, punishment, confronting young offenders with their behaviour and reinforcing the responsibilities of parents. Although there may be some conflict between those keen to enforce court orders strictly and consistently and others, such as those social workers, who, in spite of the difficulties mentioned above, continue to stress the importance of constructive work with young offenders, the overall effect of current youth justice policy and practice is correctional early intervention, deterrence and punishment. The well-established diversionary policies and practices of the 1980s have been abandoned along with genuine alternatives to incarceration (Goldson, 2000). The punishment model remains dominant, despite those who argue that we should now talk of corporatist/managerialist approaches rather than get involved in the 'old' welfare/treatment and punishment debates (Muncie, 1999). Admittedly, managerialism does reign in the sense that the focus on bureaucracy and targets has undermined the discretion and creativity of practitioners, but this does not mean that punishment is not at the fore of what happens to young people offenders.

The blurring of roles in YOTs raises similar concerns to those posed by social workers having to work so closely with the police in child protection cases. Again, the fear is that social workers will lose their professional identity. Souhami (2007, p 182) writes that 'the tone of repudiation and disdain in the communications surrounding the implementation of the Crime and Disorder Act and the radical reorganisation these set in train were understood by social workers as a dismissal of their previous practice'. What is more, despite the undoubted successes of the 1980s, social workers were criticised for being 'inactive, collusive, and ineffective ... their professional experience and expertise now appeared to count for nothing'. Additionally, when one looks at many recent texts on youth justice (for example, Goldson and Muncie, 2006; Smith, 2007; Stephenson et al, 2007) a striking observation is that social work in relation to young offending is barely mentioned. Indeed, when restorative justice and mediation are referred to in the media they are usually put forward as a police initiative, rather than the result of social work initiatives in the 1980s. Admittedly, the case is different in Scotland where social work with young offenders remains a significant aspect of dealing with youth crime (White, 2009). This is also highlighted in the edited collection by McIvor and Raynor (2007), as the title of their book refers to 'developments in *social work* with offenders'. But even they have to acknowledge the impact on social work of the abolition of the social work qualification for probation officers. In any case, whereas once social work was seen as pivotal to responding to young offenders, along with those at risk of offending, this is no longer the case, particularly in England and Wales. Perhaps the most obvious manifestation of this is that services for young people in trouble have been separated from mainstream children and families services. This separation is epitomised by *The Children Act Now: messages from research* (Aldgate and Statham, 2001), which does not even refer to young offenders. Furthermore, while eligibility criteria for statutory child welfare was tightened and social care accordingly stringently rationed, the youth offending apparatus greatly expanded under New Labour (Goldson, 2007).

New Labour and social work with adults and older people

As we saw in Chapter Three, care management came to dominate social work with adults and older people under Thatcherism and this continued under New Labour. Care management involves different approaches to different service user groups. For instance, a multi-professional model distinguishes high-risk mental health services, and a model of service brokerage has been developed to meet the needs of adults with disabilities with a defined professional role being implied in each (Payne, 2000). However, the model that has come to dominate work with older people is one of social care entrepreneurship, with the availability of services tightly constrained by cost and linked to the marketisation of social care more generally (Lymbery, 2004b). In fact, the inadequacy of the resource base has been an ongoing concern and is now certainly the most significant factor facing social work and social care with older people (Lymbery, 2010).

The concern with rationing financial resources has resulted in social workers facing increased levels of bureaucratisation, even to the extent that some argue that it signals the demise of social work with older people (Postle, 2001). This is because an overemphasis on assessment to the exclusion of other elements of care management such as monitoring and review can fragment the process, thereby leading to a number of problems. These include routinised working, resulting in swift assessments together with unimaginative planning and cursory review; large caseloads with an emphasis on processing lots of work rather than user outcomes; a proliferation of forms for various aspects of practice; the splitting of tasks between different workers, leading to general deskilling; too much of an emphasis on formal services rather than linking formal and informal services; and discouragement of the counselling and interpersonal aspects of social work (Sturges, 1996)[5]. In brief, care management has a proceduralised and bureaucratised orientation that has led to an increase in the power of managers over social workers. This is because the emphasis is on managing scarce resources rather than meeting needs. As in the Thatcherite era, New Labour saw financial imperatives as being at the fore of public services, with managers as the key players.

As well as continuing with care management, New Labour pushed forward changes in relation to personalisation. SCIE, at the behest of New Labour, has been advocating for its implementation for some time. Co-production is another element in this and, although perhaps less familiar, it is concerned with ways of creating support systems that value partnership between all parties. SCIE argues that both originate from social work values such as respect for the individual and self-determination. Another argument is that direct payments (discussed more fully in Chapter Six) and independent budgeting, which are linked to personalisation, have their roots in the service-user movement and the social model of disability, with notions of participation, control, choice and empowerment being to the fore. This is because the individual is seen as best placed to know what they need and how those needs can be met. It means that people can be responsible for themselves and make their own decisions about what they require. All this is presented as good risk management because knowing the people in someone's network of family and friends better prevents neglect and abuse. Strong communities are presented as an antidote to cultures of abuse, which are more likely to develop in care settings and more isolated corners of society.

Actually, as Ferguson (2008) notes, personalisation did not emerge from within social work or service users but from Demos, the New Labour think-tank. It is also linked to the notion of consumerism and draws on the community care reforms of the Thatcher period and the development of care management. There is a real danger of an abdication of responsibility and the juxtaposed empowerment with *abandonment*. Surely choice and control should not be promoted at the expense of safety and dignity? A policy of 'cash for care' rather than any genuine move to personalisation seems to be the goal and is more evidence of New Labour's ideological adherence to the market economy. Moreover, following the global recession of 2008-10, Demos went on to argue that personalisation could be used to combat forthcoming cuts in public spending. It added that the question of how public services can meet people's needs at lower cost will be the most pressing public policy issue for the next decade. Finally, although personalisation may be sold on the basis that it provides 'choice' and 'independence', the underlying policy agenda is more about reducing expenditure, maximising the care provided by family, friends and neighbours and thereby minimising the need for state-funded support. Indeed, one of the contributors to Hunter and Ritchie's volume *Co-production and Personalisation in Social Care* (2007, p 36) states: 'It is essential that the informal system of family and friends is supported to the greatest possible extent ... the strong value-for-money evidence for [this] approach constitutes a compelling business case'.

In summary, the argument goes, dependence on the state is to be discouraged and independence celebrated. However, this so-called independence amounts to being dependent on the market, despite all the insecurities and anxieties this brings (Leonard, 1997). The negative aspects of dependence on the market are particularly pertinent during the current global recession. Paradoxically, however, such dependency is to be lauded. The resulting public policy is concerned with shaping the choices people make about their lives so as to reduce the risk of them making expensive demands on public services. Individuals have to take more responsibility for finding their own solutions, including assessing and managing the risks of their own behaviour. This includes being liable for managing their own care within clear financial and service constraints, and even identifying their own resources in order to do so. It is not hard to see that this is where consumerism and in turn personalisation comes in. Unfortunately, however, bureaucratic processes dominate so as to manage resources and risk, rather than promote the rights and needs of service users and carers. Self-reliance and responsibility, rather than collective provision, come to the fore.

But how can it be possible to reconstruct people who rely on social work/social care as 'customers' or 'consumers' when most ordinary people lack the basic information to make meaningful choices? Furthermore, even if such information and genuine choices existed, it is far from clear that choice itself is people's primary consideration; nearness, or ease of access, to the particular service concerned is likely to be a major factor. Surely we should also step back and question the view that personalisation should increasingly be the backbone on which social care is built and provided. Being blunt, it should not be up to the individual user to sort out their own problems and difficulties, even if some, in many ways limited, help and advice is provided.

Conclusion

New Labour continued and intensified the ideological and political offensive of Thatcherism. Responsibility for meeting need is increasingly left to the individual as the state retreats from provision of services in the common interest to encouraging individuals to pursue their own interests as they see best, notwithstanding the problems this can cause them. This allows the private and voluntary sectors to play an increasing role in the provision of services. To the extent that services are provided by the state, they are subject to continued 'reform' and 'modernisation', including highly developed systems of monitoring, to ensure that standards are maintained and improved so as to meet 'consumer' demand. This coincides with a rejection of the traditional analysis of social problems in terms of structural divisions of class, 'race', gender and others. Welfare politics is more about giving everyone a fair chance rather than the redistribution of wealth. The overall 'outcome is a move to market competition, to harnessing the egoism that is understood to drive human behaviour and to an increasing rejection of state welfare collectivism' (Taylor-Gooby, 2000, p 335).

In this context, social work's role in society has become circumscribed and limited to a residual fulfilment of statutory functions (Lymbery and Butler, 2004). Under New Labour, it has been reduced to bureaucratic, standardised and largely technocratic approaches focusing on the management of risk, even though there is more to the management of risk than procedure and protocol (Broadhurst and Hall, 2009). Social work is essentially a professional activity requiring skilled, situation-specific analyses of particular cases. It is a contingent and negotiated pursuit requiring skilled relationship-based work. Top-down enactment of procedures and electronic technologies significantly constrains practice because at its heart are a range of moral rationalities to do with care, trust, kindness and respect, all of which can stray significantly from the simple calculation of the negatives or positives of this or that decision or action.

Adherence to neoliberalism, including the private sector's managerial ethos, has amounted to the deprofessionalisation of social work, which brings me to the so-called professionalisation of social work, which is the subject of the next chapter.

Notes

[1] My experience suggests that agencies have always worked together and colleagues in different agencies are often on first name terms with each other. Far from these being 'cosy' relationships, they enable genuine partnerships to develop that are more successful than New Labour's more bureaucratised attempts to introduce collaboration. Also note the Audit Commission's (2008) negative remarks about children's trusts, the successor to social services departments – this is discussed further in Chapter Seven.

[2] Deskilling is linked to deprofessionalisation, which is taken up in Chapter Five.

[3] Quality Protects was launched in 1998 with 8, later expanded to 11, key objectives aimed at, for example, creating better educational opportunities and ensuring secure and lasting attachments. In typical New Labour fashion, a number of sub-objectives, targets and performance indicators was added (see Smith, 2008, pp 108-9 for a discussion).

[4] I well recall that in the late 1970s I had to repeatedly challenge colleagues for using the derogatory term 'problem families' – surely such people are families with problems, the casualties of a fundamentally unjust economic, political and social system.

[5] The reader will not be surprised to note that many of the points raised equally apply to social work with children and families.

FIVE

The professionalisation of social work?

As we saw in Chapter Two, social work never had restricted entry to its ranks; nor did it involve a lengthy period of training, have its own body of knowledge or an element of autonomy in regulating members, all of which were common to medicine and law. Even at its 1970s peak, it was denied full professional status, despite its attempts to develop new ideas about professional identity, not always in keeping with the more orthodox definition of professionalism. For example, radical social workers of the 1970s were simply against professionalism, seeing it as elitist and more concerned with increasing the status and power of social workers themselves rather than that of service users (Simpkin, 1983). Then again, the profession was formed and dominated by women, who were often more interested in involving users in improving their lives rather than increasing their own status in the process (Dominelli, 2009a).

It is no coincidence that it was during the social democratic period that social work flourished; it was part of the welfarist project whereby national growth and well-being was seen as involving notions of mutuality and social solidarity, with social problems being ameliorated through the agency of the state and including professional intervention by social workers (Parton, 1996b). Leaving aside arguments about whether professionalism itself is a good thing, these developments highlight the increasing professionalisation of social work. There was a concern with knowledge and understanding, even though at times this included relying on other disciplines for a knowledge base. In addition, it involved more than just the practicalities of practice, the 'what' and 'how' of social work. This can be contrasted with developments since that period, which have consisted of the introduction of the Diploma in Social Work

(DipSW) by the Conservatives, followed by the onset of the social work degree together with various other post-qualifying courses under New Labour. Then there are the Social Work TaskForce's (2009) recommendations, which include social work ultimately being a master's degree profession. At first sight, these changes seem progressive, appearing to amount to the continued ongoing development of professional social work. However, the associated emphasis on competencies, together with increasing comments from politicians about how 'practical' the job is, has become a substitute for knowledge and understanding. This amounts to the deprofessionalisation of social work, which can be related to the neoliberal project, resulting in the questioning of professionalism and the need for it to be controlled by the growth of managerialism.

In this chapter I begin with some general comments about professionalism and professionalisation. I then turn to the social work education in the UK, which includes the rise and fall of the psychoanalytic approach and the influence of radicalism, which led to the employers taking over social work education. Second, I look at the role of the state, the Central Council for the Education and Training in Social Work (CCETSW) and the academy. Both draw on important work by Jones (1996) and Webb (1996) in highlighting and analysing the changes to social work education and training over the Thatcher/Major years. Third, there is a discussion of the current state of social work education and training after 13 years of New Labour. I argue that what we have witnessed is the continued deprofessionalisation of social work owing to the emphasis on discrete technical competencies in a culture that promotes market forces, consumerism and managerialism, all at the expense of fundamental aspects of social work (Lishman, 2009).

Professionalism, professionalisation and social work

In examining professionalism, professionalisation and social work, a useful starting point is the meaning of professional social work itself. In my view, professional social work covers a number of things. First, it consists of a balance of knowledge and understanding, underpinned by skills and values, all gained from education and training, that assist the social worker in undertaking the role of enabler, and at times protector, of individuals, families, groups and communities (Charnley et al, 2009). Second, it involves a concern with social justice and social change, and the ability to relate to and engage with people, assess situations and needs, plan the way forward and then ensure the implementation and review of progress. Furthermore, all this must to be done with the user so that power and responsibility are shared. Finally, social work is about building alliances, and combining knowledge and skills so as to benefit the user. All this is uncontroversial and will appeal to most, apart from those on the political left and right.

I have already referred to the 1970s' radical critique of professionalism and professionalisation of social work, which centred on the elitist aspects of privileging the ambitions of social workers rather than service users. Another important point was that it privileged social workers against other, less qualified, workers. However, during the 1980s, attacks on professional power, or 'producer power' as it was called, came from the New Right. This view sees politicians and consumers having limited power, with services being geared to the needs of producers rather than the public interest or the needs of users (George and Wilding, 1994). There were no mechanisms to ensure that services developed in response to changing needs or proven deficiencies, so it was in the interests of the producers to preserve the status quo. What the New Right was really concerned about, however, was that the welfare state offered few opportunities to private companies to make profits (Ferguson and Woodward, 2009). It used the language of 'empowering users and carers' to create a 'mixed economy of care' so as to extend 'choice', all of which created opportunities for private companies. At the forefront of this process was an increase in managerial power (see Chapter Six) with a resulting questioning and reduction of the professional autonomy of social workers evidenced by various deprofessionalising tendencies.

Moreover, now that neoliberalism is the dominant global ideology of the new millennium, it is worth revisiting the 1970s radical critique, even if somewhat defensively. In the first place, deprofessionalisation, which is implicit in that critique, increases gender inequality in the public sector because it increasingly draws more working-class and women from minority ethnic communities into the labour force. Arguing against professionalisation in this scenario merely marginalises these women even further. Then there is the fact that 'old' radical critiques resonate all too well with neoliberal imperatives that see professional knowledge and skill as unnecessary and even inconsistent with good social work practice (Healy and Meagher, 2004). For example, if responsibilities and the work involved can be broken down into smaller, easier tasks, less knowledge, understanding and skill is required almost to the extent that, it could be argued, 'anyone' can do them. The counter-argument, of course, is that poorly trained and supported workers are less likely to be able to carry out thoughtful, analytic and creative social work, and deprofessionalised workers are less likely to be in a position to defend the interests of users, especially when such interests are counter to current organisational and policy dictates. As Ferguson and Woodward (2009, p 148) put it: '[This] argument is a strong one and one that is likely to strike a chord with many social workers in Britain, after almost two decades during which both social work education and social work practice have been dominated by the needs and requirements of employers, and personal relationships with clients increasingly replaced by what are essentially commercial relationships with service users or "customers"'.

There are two other points to note here. The first relates to the inherent tension between social workers' understanding of professionalism, which includes the knowledge, understanding, skills and values they bring to the job, and the completely different knowledge and value base that informs the managerialism that now prevails and needs to be resisted. The second point is that, as we shall see, although the user movement challenges the more orthodox notion of professionalism, this certainly does not mean that it should be abandoned. Rather, the challenge is 'to develop forms of professionalism which are consistent with, and welcoming of, user participation and a commitment to equality and social justice – that is, professionalism based on partnership' (Thompson, 2002, p 717). Surrendering social work's claims to professionalism and professionalisation falls into the hands of neoliberals who would like to see the wholesale destruction of professional social work. If one looks at the recent development of social work education in Britain, this is precisely what can be seen.

Social work education

Following the influence of Thatcherism, there are two important points to note about social work education in Britain (Jones, 1996). First, because social work is a contested domain concerning how people live and manage their lives and interact with the state and one another, you might expect diversity in social work education, reflecting different perspectives and views of the world. However, nothing could be further from the truth, simply because of the tightness of external regulation of social work courses. Second, since the 1970s, there has been a prevailing hostility towards social science's concern with knowledge and understanding; instead, there is an emphasis on skills and competencies, which fit more easily with the needs of employers. Admittedly, there are some that see the distinction between knowledge and understanding, and skills and competencies as somewhat artificial (Cree and Myers, 2008). However, surely conceptual knowledge – theories, propositions and facts – actually enable understanding and is different to procedural and professional knowledge – knowing respectively *how* to do things and what skills are needed, and knowing *about* personal and social work values. The very fact that neoliberal governments distrust a social work practice that relies on theory attests to this. At any rate, the extent of external regulation of social work courses and the hostility to social science can be seen as part of the neoliberal suspicion of welfare professions that are often seen as encouraging dependency. In addition, such issues have continuity with the ongoing construction and development of social work education and training since the 19th century.

Social work has always been seen as an activity that risks the contamination of those working with the most disadvantaged in society because they might start seeing things from the standpoint of the poor rather than the rich. This can cause problems for authority, as the context of practice has always been one that can sustain a perspective that sees human suffering as the result of inequalities rather than individual or family pathology. This was one of the factors influencing social work education, along with the need to prevent social workers' demoralisation resulting from daily contact with deprived and impoverished sections of society. Early social work education by the Charity Organisation Society included 'knowledge' that endorsed the prevailing social order based on liberalism and Judeo-Christian beliefs. After the Second World War, the political climate was such that a social work practice based on religious or overtly moralistic tones was no longer acceptable. Instead, the language of scientific rationality, expertise and professionalism came to the fore, leading to theories, perspectives and research findings from social science being utilised and adapted so as to construct modern social work's knowledge base (Wootton, 1959). The targets for this pragmatic and eclectic approach were social workers as well as wider society. However, continued poverty and human suffering, even in more affluent societies, meant that state social work remained a deeply contested activity. Arguments by the powerful that the causation of problems and difficulties resided within individuals and families, rather than being as the result of societal pressures, left social workers in a difficult position. It is no surprise that their preparation and socialisation was given attention.

During the 1950s and 1960s, while critical work from sociology and social policy were marginalised on social work courses, Freudian psychology in the form of psychoanalysis or versions of it allowed social work to have a semblance of theoretical coherence. Psychoanalysis resonated with social democratic concerns with social reform and allowed the possibility of everyone achieving citizenship. It broke with earlier biological theorising on poverty and inequality whereby the undeserving poor were eugenically unfit or biologically incapable of being rehabilitated. It also provided social work with a much-needed scientific credibility (Bailey and Brake, 1975). Importantly, only those aspects of the Freudian tradition that reinforced personal and familial pathology as the root of social problems tended to feature on social work courses, not those that posed a more critical psychology such as that of Marcuse (1964), which combined Marxist and Freudian perspectives.

The dominance of psychoanalysis proved short-lived as the economic and fiscal crisis of the mid-1970s proved damaging to social work and public expenditure was cut. Many practitioners also found the pressure of working within the large, impersonal bureaucracy of social services departments (SSDs) difficult to cope with as they were bombarded with referrals not directly from users but rather 'from an array of state and public authorities who were exploiting the formation of a single agency to off-load their problematic and time-consuming tenants/pupils/patients/claimants/debtors and so forth' (Jones, 1996, p 198). In such a situation it was hard to reconcile undertaking a casework approach informed by psychoanalysis, which, given the emphasis on the therapeutic relationship, demands time and cooperation from the user. Furthermore, even in the 1970s administrators, and soon managers, were being increasingly pressed to deliver services efficiently and thereby provide 'value for money' rather than be guided by the ideals of public service. Such changes were certainly not conducive to pursuing psychoanalytically based casework.

As social policy moved to the right, social work education and practice was feeling the impact of the radical and critical currents that confronted many western societies during the late 1960s and early 1970s. The expansion of higher education saw many social science graduates attracted to social work. Influenced by the social movements of the time, as well as their previous education that had exposed them to emerging radical insights in subjects such as philosophy, sociology, social policy and psychology, they questioned the traditional, individualised tenets of social work. A common strand was questioning traditional authority and associated 'truths'. Important social policy texts saw poverty as a feature of capitalism rather than the moral malfunction of particular problem families; critical social psychology in the form of work by Laing (for example, 1965) and Marcuse (1964), and in many feminists writings, questioned the sanctity of the patriarchal family; and the 'new' deviancy theorists (see Taylor et al, 1973) questioned the nature of deviance and the role of the state and state professionals, including social workers, in reproducing deviance. From such diverse standpoints, the mainstream social work view that society, despite its flaws, was concerned about the welfare of all its citizens was seriously challenged. The expansion of state social work, the collapse of psychoanalytically based casework

---

both as knowledge base and method, and the radical/critical turn was a profoundly heady mix, and was to have unforeseen and damaging consequences (Jones, 1996).

One view was that whereas the social sciences had once been looted to provide support for traditional social work, they were now, at least in their radical form, seen to be dangerous and threatening. This was because they suggested some real possibilities for practice, whereby the concerns of users were paramount. It was not just that the latter were seen as casualties or victims of an unjust economic, social and political system, but also that the role of the state and of its social workers was problematised. State welfare professionalism, which had flourished under social democracy, was seen as anti-democratic and unaccountable, with in-built paternalism and inequalities. As indicated, a key component of the radical critique was that the professionals, as a result of their education and training, were deemed to be the experts who defined the problems and solutions, whereas users, as non-specialists, were seen as having few rights in defining needs or solutions. As a result, anti-professionalism became a key feature of social work during the 1970s whereby social workers and clients became allies in the pursuit of social justice. This might seem rather naive and idealistic today, but nevertheless serious attention was being given to developing alternative ways of working utilising radical, feminist and progressive political perspectives. The traditional social work academy had difficulty in countering such views as well as the ensuing serious questions in relation to society, families, gender relations, sexuality and racism. Unfortunately, the vacuum that emerged enabled the employers to step in and to take over.

The bureaucratisation of SSDs and the upsurge of radicalism saw employers question social work courses and the right of education institutions to determine the curriculum and ethos of social work education. The concern was that social work courses were turning out difficult employees, namely social workers who thought and acted as if they were autonomous professionals with obligations to improve, as they saw fit, the well-being of clients. The Certificate of Qualification in Social Work (CQSW) was the obvious target as the 1970s progressed, with the critique being centred on social workers being radicalised by their exposure to social science. For some, the social work strike at the end of the 1970s was evidence of this. Furthermore, whereas at the beginning of the 1970s CCETSW acknowledged the need for students to have an understanding of social action and reform, a few years later it was lamenting the fact that students and their teachers were not willing to compromise their principles on such issues (see Jones, 1996, p 205). Throughout the 1980s, CCETSW became the site of engagement, with successive Conservative governments committed to increasing the representation of business and employers so as to ensure that it regulated and shaped social work education in the interests of employers who wanted social workers to 'do' rather than think. Such discussions culminated in the CQSW being replaced by the Diploma in Social Work in 1989. It is no coincidence that by 1990, as Brewster (1992, p 88) pointed out, the composition of the council saw representation from higher education finally eclipsed by the 'new managers', going on to state that it had become a perfect vehicle for the enterprise of Thatcherism. From then on, under pressure from employers and successive Conservative governments, CCETSW gradually removed the centrality of social science disciplines from the curriculum and the control of education institutions over professional courses. Ministers demeaned theorisation as 'fashionable', instead demanding 'common sense' for what was considered a practical job. Training and competencies were what was required rather than education, research, knowledge and understanding.

CCETSW and the academy

The role of CCETSW, in Webb's (1996, p 175) words the 'legitimator and definer of social work knowledge and skills', in regulating and controlling social work training was pivotal for the 30 years of its existence. Its work may have started out a little like the product of a genteel debate among the wise and good about the desirable aspects of qualifying training, but it increasingly became answerable to government as an instrument for policy control over skill mix and workforce governance, and in so doing it became an extension of employers' interests. These changes are exemplified in the developments in relation to CCETSW's Paper 30 (CCETSW, 1989), which referred to the 'endemic racism' in British society and can be analysed in terms of three interlinked domains: the stipulation of practice competence by means of a discourse around 'training'; the requirement of demonstrable moral conduct towards social oppression; and, by insisting on 'partnership' in delivering social work, the decentring of the academy as the location within which social work knowledge is set (Webb, 1996).

A key point is that CCETSW operated as a quasi-non-governmental body that operated with the permission of the government departments that funded it. This in turn constructs the way social work education was and is formed and the practices and knowledge that are permissible. Given that social work includes monitoring and controlling what the Victorians called 'dangerous and threatening aggregates', social workers needed to become reliable state agents, with CCETSW necessarily having to play its part in ensuring this. In addition, as neoliberalism has dominated since the late 1970s, it has had to operate within and facilitate the neoliberal project.

The emphasis on training and competencies had a significant impact on CCETSW's regulatory project. Until the introduction of the Diploma in Social Work, the training requirements for professional education were relatively permissive and gave scope for an emphasis on knowledge rather than simple competencies. This gave the academy space to develop the curriculum without having to give undue weight to narrow technical proficiency. This independence caused obvious problems for CCETSW, which found it difficult to exert control over what was being taught. It therefore reached the stage when it had to assert itself by breaking the autonomy of the academy in order to ensure its own future.

From the early 1970s onwards, there were frequently articulated and politically orchestrated public expressions about the competence of social workers along with attacks on those who happened to be in the clutches of such 'do-gooders'[1]. Various child abuse inquiries contributed to this, while others criticised social work's preoccupation with social change. All this added to the increasing destabilisation of the whole enterprise of social work education, which reached a head during Thatcher's tenure.

During the mid-1980s, CCETSW, intent on a more robust role and hence more government support, saw employer-led initiatives in relation to vocational education more widely as the way forward. The academy, the argument went, had to heed the voice of the 'consumer', and 'partnership' was to be the tool to bring the colleges into line. This partly involved the Certificate of Social Service being promoted as equivalent to professional education, even though this was never meant to be the case. The certificate had been introduced in 1977 as an in-service route for social services staff and featured joint management arrangements that saw social work agencies involved in determining the nature and content of education and training. Because of these partnership arrangements, in effect it emerged as the model for the future Diploma in Social Work. In Webb's (1996, p 181) words, 'CCETSW would bring the querulous secular clerics of a recalcitrant academy into line and at the same time offer a way to restructure the welfare workforce through a realignment of the training and education mix'. CCETSW thereby became an enthusiastic example of social work's own post-Fordism of flexibility, decentralisation and market plurality. According to Webb (1996, p 181), 'it "appeared" to loosen its direct control over education, creating instead pseudo-autonomous programme providers operating as quasi-businesses founded on semi-contractual mutual partnerships in order to meet the "specifications" set by the Council'. These changes can be seen as aspects of the shift in the relative weighting given to education and training in social work, particularly the emphasis on specifying the tasks to be done rather than the knowledge to be gained, and had several consequences. They enabled a strategy for control of both employees and of education, since the contracts for delivery are capable of high degrees of precision. Skills become less tied to one particular job and could be transferred across settings and boundaries that used to be set by the practices of occupational and professional power. Differentiation of task also leads to fragmentation of activity and an increase in the subordination of welfare workers, including social workers, to the tightly specified concerns of employers.

Parallel with the regulatory character of DipSW, with its emphasis on highly prescriptive competencies, was a wider set of directives affecting social work education. These related to anti-oppressive practice and, though superficially radical, the approach to such values still existed within a performance-oriented discourse set in a similar mode to the other competencies that had to be demonstrated by social workers. In addition, CCETSW's pronouncements about oppression were carried out within a discourse that saw the abandonment of class and the depoliticising of resistance. It was also unconnected with any account of causation or of the interrelationship between social categories such as class itself, gender, 'race' and so on. Simply embracing concepts such as 'diversity' and 'difference' sounds rather hollow if unaccompanied by an understanding that the creation of inequality and division is a consequence of economic and government processes. Simultaneously, there was an inherent instability within all this, evidenced by CCETSW having to withdraw the declaration about 'endemic racism' in British society in the original regulations for the DipSW (CCETSW, 1989). Such comments were not well received in certain quarters, notably ministerial circles, and the offending words were removed relatively easily precisely because CCETSW had excluded the social sciences, and thereby the social scientists, that could have shown empirically that racism, as well as other oppressions, *is* structurally endemic. However, as CCETSW had failed to acknowledge the complexities in conceptualising oppression, it found itself unable to defend its position. Since its approach to anti-discrimination was framed around competencies to the exclusion of analysis and knowledge, it was epistemologically unstable, hence the ease with which the 'endemic racism' passage was removed.

Throughout the Thatcher/Major years, social work education was noticeably reframed, with education being supplanted by training, discourses of depth being replaced by those of surface and knowledge being set aside for competencies which have triumphed over the complexities of abstraction. This was all about shaping anew the definition of what passes for social work as a practical and conceptual activity. For all its statements about combating oppression, CCETSW effectively agreed to relationships that were consonant with those of conservative modernisation. Its structural position was set firmly within what Althusser (1971) referred to as the ideological state apparatus, with superficial exhortations to repudiate discrimination in effect sitting alongside an approval of neoliberalism.

As well as an endorsement of neoliberalism and hence modernity, the role of CCETSW also had features that were postmodern. Mention has already been made of it being a good example of post-Fordism with its concern with flexibility and decentralisation. The increased emphasis on doing tasks rather than gaining knowledge also highlights a key point already mentioned. This is the move from the in-depth explanations of modernity's concern with transcendent truth to postmodern concerns with the multiplicities of superficial performance. There is an absence of deep structure, about causes, for example, in the moral discourse about anti-oppression because it was primarily framed within the superficiality of rhetoric and competencies. There is also an erasing or obscuring of complexity, together with a reluctance to consider the links between oppressions, which instead become rendered as competing, almost individualistic characteristics. There is also the associated imagery that oppressions can somehow be chosen, displayed almost as in a market for selection (see Webb, 1996, pp 185-6).

Finally, it is worth noting that introduction of the DipSW did many things that were consistent with CCETSW's overt and covert objectives. First, it was an expression of anti-intellectualism that had its revenge on an academy that was unable or unwilling to bring the radicals within social work into line. Second, CCETSW was able to demonstrate to government that it could deliver reliably within the employer-led ethos of vocational training, thereby ensuring trustworthy and predictable welfare workers whose previous unpredictability, unreliability and autonomy were the source of ills they should have been solving. And third, CCETSW served as the body for integrating new and sometimes troublesome entrants to social work. All in all, CCETSW was 'the instrument for securing the *dirigiste* restructuring of professional training through reframing professional social work as a flexible, technically specific (and highly specified) enterprise in which skill-mix considerations are put to work at the behest of employers' (Webb, 1996, p 188, emphasis in original). Its more progressive utterances were to be changed, and even the more radical pronouncements in relation to endemic racism were more superficial than substantial. Although all this amounted

---

to attempts to ensure CCETSW's survival, in reality it only delayed its demise.

New Labour, new professionalisation?

As highlighted in Chapter Four, the election of a New Labour government in 1997 brought with it a requirement for the 'modernisation' of public services, including social services and social work, which was generally accepted as meaning they should become more business-like. One has only to witness the emphasis on modernisation and reform following the White Paper *Modernising Social Services* (DH, 1998), which resulted in changes to the social care landscape largely as a result of the 2000 Care Standards Act and the introduction of new regulatory and inspection regimes (Lymbery, 2004a). The aim was to strengthen social services, but importantly it often resulted in social work as a distinct profession being subsumed by the more general category of 'social care'.

More positive, and perhaps the most significant development under New Labour as far as professionalism is concerned, was the introduction of the new social work BA degree introduced in 2003/04, along with social workers being granted a 'protected title' by registering with the General Social Care Council every three years after having shown they have undertaken 90 hours of continuous professional development. The degree is based on the National Occupational Standards for Social Work (TOPPS, 2002), as was its predecessor, the DipSW. Ostensibly these standards provide a set of descriptions of the functions of social workers and aim to provide a benchmark of 'best practice' in social work competence across the UK (Cree and Myers, 2008). They were developed from an analysis of what social workers do, through consultation with employers and practitioners, and included users' views of their expectations of social workers.

The first point to note, however, is that employers and New Labour were dissatisfied with educators being unable to produce social workers who on completion of the DipSW could not turn up at the office and carry out the job without the need for further training and supervision (Dominelli, 2009a). The introduction of the degree was an attempt to deal with this by increasing the amount of time spent on practice placements to 100 days a year. However, the government did not provide the funds for local authorities to provide high-quality placements and importantly the qualification in practice teaching was no longer compulsory. Merely increasing the time on placement was unlikely to achieve what the employers wanted unless they simply felt that at least this meant less time was spent on 'irrelevant' theory.

More fundamentally, perhaps, the DipSW was subject to criticism, as earlier comments suggest. In brief, it emphasised social work training rather than education, took a narrow view of what social work is, and had the potential to undermine practitioners' autonomy and flexibility with its competence-based approach (Ferguson and Woodward, 2009). In some ways, the new degree can be seen as an attempt to tackle the complex nature of the social work role and task together with its increasing association with social care. Instead of DipSW's 26 single competencies, the new degree is based on a set of standards each requiring that students demonstrate not only that they have gained competence in a particular area but also that they have acquired set knowledge and skills. To ensure that students are able to achieve the new standards, academic institutions must still deliver a prescribed degree programme based on set teaching, learning and assessment requirements in relation to, for instance, service user and carer involvement, and integrated working practices.

While there is some scope for locally negotiated agreements about the content and delivery of degree programmes, generally the knowledge, skills and even value base that educators must teach, and students must acquire, remains externally imposed. This would be fine if everyone were in agreement about what good social work and social work education is, but, as pointed out earlier, this is a contested area. Also, developing a good curriculum requires educators to consider more than the requirements of external agencies or internal quality procedures. Students' needs and their time and research interests, for example, need consideration. At the very least, competence-based approaches need to be combined with more creative and critical approaches so as to ensure that education is not just a matter of training by numbers. Lecturers sometimes struggle to cover all aspects of the degree *and* to help students to think critically and creatively, while students themselves have few opportunities to develop their own interests and ways of practice (Ferguson and Woodward, 2009).

On the one hand, the successor to DipSW can be seen as increasing the professionalism of social work to degree level, but on the other, it is still preoccupied with turning out reliable and compliant workers who will simply, and largely unthinkingly, bend to the will of employers through their managers. This is evidenced by the fact that the degree focuses on social workers gaining practical skills (DH, 2002) rather than the kind of knowledge that will help combat social injustice. While academics as a whole welcomed the move to a graduate profession, they were certainly less than enthused about the new degree's increased reliance on 'mechanistic skills' and a 'competence model of education' (Orme et al, 2009). The New Right may well not have held on to the ideal that social work can be used as a unifying force within society, instead imposing on it a more restrictive, coercive and closely managed role devoid of any real measure of professional autonomy. Similarly, New Labour, continuing with these neoliberal ideas, was resistant to the label of 'professional' or even the words 'social work' during most of its tenure of office.

In fact, there is an element of anti-intellectualism in New Labour's approach to social work education, despite the degree's introduction. This is because the degree does not necessarily lend itself to the kind of intellectual work that is centred on knowledge, understanding, skills and values, which in turn refer to what the social worker must 'know' and 'do' and 'should be'. One only has to witness New Labour politicians' repeated derogatory, anti-intellectual comments about social work. In early 2009, at the height of the controversy over Baby Peter, Ed Balls, the then Secretary of State for Children, Families and Schools, commented that social work training was too theoretical because it was a practical job, even implying that all that was needed to do it was 'common sense'. Moreover, Jacqui Smith, as a minister of state, also said social work was 'a very practical job. It is about protecting people and changing their lives, not being able to give fluent, theoretical explanations of why they got into difficulties in the first place' (cited in Ferguson and Woodward, 2009, p 154).

However, knowledge, ideas, understanding and hence theory are essential components of practice. As well as being engaged in the critical appraisal of policy and management initiatives, it has to involve an intellectual understanding of both the strengths and weaknesses of the work being done and of alternative ways of working. Surely it is exactly because social work has become so bureaucratic, standardised and watered down by the overall social care agenda that it is essential to emphasise that good social work is not, and cannot be, simply *common sense*.

Continuing professional(?) development

After introducing the social work degree, New Labour went on to re-emphasise continuing professional development (CPD) and the new post-qualifying (PQ) courses. In a beguiling chapter, Higham (2009, p 8) asks whether these developments amount to 'flagships for social work reform or sinking ships'?

The previous framework for PQ was established in 1991 and offered two award levels managed by regional post-qualifying consortia, although they were diverted from a key task of strategic workforce planning. The most successful programme was PQ1, consolidation of qualifying level competencies, but most social workers did not progress beyond this to complete a full award. Standardisation was also difficult to achieve, as the consortia worked independently of each other. As a result, the UK-wide PQ awards were phased out from 2007, with England's new framework beginning in autumn of that year, followed by those in Scotland, Wales and Northern Ireland in 2008. These country-specific PQ frameworks are specifically designed to promote strategic workforce and human resources planning by developing the social work workforce.

The PQ framework's curricula are strongly influenced by employers' human resources strategies, which seek to sustain the workforce's motivation and commitment as well as developing new roles and skills. Developing skills and confidence for practice within multi-professional teams was seen as being particularly necessary because such teams are characteristic of contemporary organisational structures. Taken as a whole, there were three aims:

developing practitioners beyond the beginning levels of competence in specialist areas of practice; promoting interprofessional learning and multiprofessional practice; and developing leadership and management skills. Despite this, potential impediments to the success of PQ frameworks include their complex and overregulated nature, underdeveloped workforce planning, the potential lack of portability across UK countries, cost and insufficient 'fitness for purpose' (Higham, 2009). In addition, there is no agreement on the overall purpose of PQ learning, with employers often seeing it as merely a vehicle for making social workers competent, almost a remedial programme following qualification. But surely the main purpose of PQ is professional development, which includes enhancing and updating existing knowledge and skills, and providing opportunities for reflective and analytic thinking, together with a commitment to broad CPD rather than training.

As indicated, a damaging aspect of the PQ framework is the preoccupation with evidence of 'competence', an attribute linked to practice at the point of qualification, rather than a focus on how practice can be improved beyond competence. This preoccupation does not allow for the development of practice expertise. Following Eraut (1994), 'competence' was initially a rationale for justifying professional examinations or assessments, but has now become a governmental tool for the regulatory control of professionals. A competent practitioner may be tolerably good, but they are still less than expert. Instead of competence, Eraut prefers the term 'capability', which has a wider meaning that refers to everything a person can think or do, thereby recognising that practitioners have reserves of capability beyond the limits of narrowly defined competence. It is concerned with growth and potential as well as current performance. 'Capability' thus integrates knowledge, skills, understanding and personal qualities, all entwined with a capacity for autonomous learning. Similarly, Schon (for example, 1996) has made a significant contribution to social workers' understanding of how professionals learn and develop their practice. Two kinds of reflective practice are theorised: 'reflection in action' requires practitioners to think on their feet and test ideas within practice situations, while 'reflection on action' involves considering actions of the past. Eraut and Schon can help PQ practitioners become more aware of significant aspects of practice situations, decisions and actions. Both are a welcome antidote to the more overtly PQ concerns with remedying or improving competence.

In a similar vein, MacDonald (2006) remains optimistic, even when pointing out that social workers have become marginal to policy making and as a result are less able to influence directions of practice. A danger is that while the social work degree and PQ frameworks may produce social workers who can practise within a new institutional order following New Labour's various policy and organisational changes, at the same time they may ignore social justice. PQ, MacDonald adds, opens up possibilities to help social workers develop strategies for bringing about changes that make a genuine difference to users' lives. The challenge is to move beyond the rhetoric of modernising agendas so as to see some critical, albeit slim, possibilities within policy and practice contexts.

The introduction of the social work degree and the emphasis on CPD and PQ practice have been significant developments, even if not always positive ones. However, the report of the Social Work Task Force (2009), published in response to the Baby Peter case, contains some significant proposals that may or may not influence the professionalisation of social work. The foreword (2009, p 3) acknowledges that the social work 'profession is not currently flourishing in England' and, one might add, in the other countries of the UK. Recommendations include a probationary year after graduation, a licence to practise, a career development framework, including a practice-based masters qualification, new standards for employers and a national college of social work. A Social Work Reform Board has been established to take forward these proposals and in early 2010 New Labour suggested that a General Social Work Council (GSWC) be established, focusing solely on social work with responsibility for other social care workers being transferred to a new Care Professionals Council (DH, 2010). While these changes appeared to be an endorsement of social work, the GSWC would fall under the umbrella of the Council for *Healthcare* Regulatory Excellence and its potential remains unfulfilled.

The probationary year envisages a supported and assessed first year in employment, allowing social workers to specialise in areas of work and build on the grounding provided by the degree. The licence to practice system involves practitioners first acquiring and then maintaining their status as social workers by demonstrating they have kept to standards of continuing competency and professional development. The report proposes more rigorous monitoring of this, so that tangible improvements in knowledge and skills would have to be shown. While it largely endorses the current CPD and PQ framework, the report points out that it is not valued and supported in all areas, hence the need for all employers to develop a strong learning culture evidenced by, for example, freeing up staff time for courses. Moreover, a more coherent and effective national framework for continuing professional development – one that incorporates a new master's degree in social work practice – is seen as being necessary. More broadly, employers need to agree to new standards for the support and supervision of frontline social workers, so as to make good practice possible. Finally, the college of social work is seen as being able to give the profession strong and independent leadership, a clear voice in public debate, policy development and policy delivery as well as ownership of the overall standards to be upheld.

At first sight few would quibble with many of these recommendations and they appear to continue and consolidate the ongoing professionalisation of social work. However, if one looks a little closer at the report, many of the earlier comments relating to this (so-called) professionalisation process continue to ring true. For example, although employers have certain obligations towards their workers and are expected to maintain certain standards, their power over what is being proposed remains undiminished. It is largely because they have argued that the current degree does not prepare students to immediately undertake all aspects of the job on graduating that the various changes are being suggested. Furthermore, they are urged to become even more involved in devising and delivering social work courses so that they get the social workers they want and need. It is as if social work is what employers say it is, rather than its definition emanating from within the profession itself. Added to this is the continued emphasis on competencies, notwithstanding the criticisms made earlier that this downgrades knowledge and understanding. The report also says little about the most significant factor in the problems besetting social work today, namely the dominance of the notion of managerialism imported from the private sector. Finally, the report is silent when it comes to the deprofessionalising tendencies in social work that greatly increased under New Labour, and one has only to recall that the proposal for a GSWC remains just that.

Deprofessionalising tendencies

In examining deprofessionalising tendencies in relation to social work practice, let us consider a number of service user groups: children, young people and families; people with mental health issues; older people; and people with disabilities. I will also comment on what was once a fundamental role for social workers, namely work with young offenders.

First, social workers for children, young people and families witnessed the establishment of innumerable new agencies during the New Labour years (Doyle and Kennedy, 2009). They have had to keep abreast of innumerable policy and legislative documents, as well as various paper and electronic assessment tools. Many of these developments were the consequence of inquiries into the deaths of children, notably that of Victoria Climbié, leading to the Laming report (Laming, 2003), the Every Child Matters agenda and the subsequent 2004 Children Act. A more recent example of these 'reforming' initiatives was the introduction of the Public Law Outline in 2008. This was aimed at reducing delays in the family courts through earlier intervention, greater use of pre-court assessments of parents and family members, and reducing the number of stages in the proceedings. In reality, it meant an increased burden on already hard-pressed social workers who had to continue to deliver day-to-day services while these changes and directives, together with many others, took place. Although such initiatives are often enthusiastically embraced by managers, the negative impact they usually have on practice is ignored, with many social workers pointing out that 'practice landscapes under modernising agendas had [actually] served to undo good practice (Doyle and Kennedy, 2009, p 51). As Stepney

(2006) points out, the introduction of initiatives aimed at 'reforming' public services are designed to quantify and justify service outcomes, often resulting in the policing function dominating practice objectives at the expense of other priorities, including the real needs of service users. Consequently, social workers are often so busy at 'getting (the current) job done' that they are in danger of losing sight of what and who they are, including their professional uniqueness and style of intervention; it is not hard to see that in many cases filling in forms and inputting data into computers can become the be all and end all of what they do. So-called modernising developments often lead to social workers having to work their way through a maze of new rules and procedures while simultaneously adhering to deadlines and targets to achieve organisational performance indicators. Concerns about the lack of opportunities for developing a progressive, even radical/critical practice, of working anti-oppressively, currently seem more relevant than ever.

Second, social work in relation to mental health witnessed a turbulent period following its integration into health after the break-up of social services departments (Bowl, 2009). The real danger is that an understanding of the social perspective will be undermined within organisations dominated by medical models of intervention. As a consequence of this, the value of services addressing a *social* rather than a *clinical* function can be questioned, with, for instance, day-care services being targeted for cutbacks despite being rated by users as among the most useful of resources. There has also been the creation of new roles within mental health services, including 'primary care graduate mental health workers' and 'support, time and recovery workers'. Many of their tasks are similar to those of mental health social workers and their appointment can again be seen as part of the process of deprofessionalisation, whereby trained and skilled professional workers are replaced by less trained and skilled workers. There is also the fact that multidisciplinary working is often less about ensuring more effective services from the various professionals involved and more about managers having a chance to erode distinctions between roles. Finally, the dilution of the approved social worker (ASW) role following the 2007 Mental Health Act and the introduction of an approved mental health practitioner role opened up the ASW role to nurses, occupational therapists and psychologists as well as social workers. A key concern is that the extension of the ASW role to health professionals who lack the experience and training of social models of intervention at the very least shows a lack of respect and belief in the knowledge and skills of ASWs and social work as a whole.

Third, in relation to social work practice with older people, the development of care management whereby managerialism, bureaucratisation, form filling and financial assessments dominate means that the traditional activities of social work involving a relationship-based service have largely been brought to an end (Griffiths et al, 2009). Care management can even be seen to have undermined social work itself, with the introduction of direct payments and personalisation being further nails in the coffin of social work with older people. Such developments perhaps help explain the current enthusiasm for the term 'social care' rather than 'social work'. At any rate, to the extent that any genuine social work practice remains, it is often carried out by staff with little or no qualifications (Rogowski, 2009) and is further evidence of deprofessionalisation.

Fourth, social work practice with people with disabilities is particularly at risk of deprofessionalisation. A key argument is that social workers must change from trying to be expert definers of need and rationers of services to being a resource for disabled people to use as they choose (Sapey, 2009). They should also stop being allied to medicine in favour of being allied to the community. In short, they must abandon their role as experts and become more immersed in disability culture and politics. If they do not do this, the argument continues, we could see the death of social work in relation to disabled people. Indeed, Oliver (2004, p 25) writes that 'social work has failed to meet disabled people's self-articulated needs. Twenty years ago I predicted that if social work were not prepared to change in terms of its practice towards disabled people, it would eventually disappear altogether. Given the proposed changes by the New Labour government in respect of modernising social services, it seems likely that forecast is about to come true. We can probably now announce the death of social work at least in relation to its involvement in the lives of disabled people'.

Finally, social work with young offenders is yet another casualty of deprofessionalisation. The introduction of multi-agency youth offending teams (YOTs) has meant that social work's emphasis on the young person's wider social and economic context is often lost, as the more overtly 'law-related' professions, notably the police, are more concerned with the victim/complainant and with ensuring that the offender is appropriately punished. Social work can also be seen as being tied into a system that is primarily concerned with the management of risk by controlling the behaviour of young people who represent a threat to the wider community (Smith, 2008). Professional divisions have become blurred and less distinguishable to the extent that the YOT practitioner has emerged with a uniform identity. When one considers that YOTs increasingly rely on specialist practitioners such as YOT support workers who do not have any prior agency affiliations, it is clear that the role and influence of social workers appears to be diminishing. The influence of managerialism is also apparent in the ASSET form, which practitioners have to complete for all young people entering the youth justice system. It is supposed to assist with decision making in practice but is often simply a management tool to improve information gathering (Smith, 2007; Whyte, 2009). It can also be criticised on the basis of its 'tick-box' approach, with a heavy emphasis on negative indicators of risk of offending, predisposing practitioners to a narrow and unfavourable view of the young person and their behaviour. There is also a focus on the individual or family domain, which leaves little opportunity to comment on disadvantage and exclusion being related to structural factors. This focus on very prescriptive form filling can lead to the 'zombification' of social workers in youth justice (Pitts, 2001) and is yet another example of deprofessionalisation.

Conclusion

On one level, one could argue that the fact that social work is now a graduate profession, with a 'protected title', its own code of practice and a commitment to continuing professional development, is proof of its increased professionalisation. Similarly, the establishment of social care councils (and perhaps a social work council), institutes for excellence and inspection agencies throughout the U.K., all of which seek to build a more accountable, reliable and effective workforce by way of registration, regulation, inspection and dissemination of 'good practice' initiatives, could be seen as constructive (Higham, 2006). However, as always, we must take account of the ideological, economic, social and political context in which such changes have taken place.

Neoliberals question the whole concepts of professionalism, not believing, or at the very least doubting, the notion of professional altruism whereby professional knowledge and know-how could benefit all. Instead, their critiques increasingly focus on monopolistic professional power as being an exploitative force, together with scepticism about the beneficial effects of professionalism as a strategy for collective occupational advancement or mobility. This has an affinity with postmodernism's questioning of faith in science and reason, which informs professionalism. It also includes hostility towards groups and organisations that threaten the free operation of the market. Some even see professions as the product of a collusive state–professional relationship generating structures of social control that are evidence of an advance towards socialism. It is within this context that the development of social work education and training, increasingly at the behest of the government and employers via their managers, has to be viewed.

New Labour continued the New Right's privatisation and marketisation of services, together with ever more managerial control over social work practice. Social workers and their practice are no longer judged on their own terms, but rather on the criteria and rules of management (Green, 2009). Regardless of the continued rhetoric about the need for increased professionalisation, and actions such as the introduction of the social work degree and PQ framework that ostensibly support this rhetoric, we have actually witnessed the deprofessionalisation of social work. Whereas nobody would disagree with the need to have an accountable and effective workforce, there is surely some debate to be had about whether increased monitoring, standardisation and regulation, both in terms of education and training as well as practice, is actually the best way to achieve this for practitioners or, more importantly, service users.

Mention of privatisation, marketisation and managers brings me to 'managerialism' and 'the social work business', which together form the title of the next chapter.

Note

[1] Such comments continue to the present time – witness, for example, the press and media hysteria following the death of Baby Peter. This is discussed further in Chapter Seven.

SIX

Managerialism and the social work business

The influence of managers and managerialism in social work has featured heavily in this book and I make no apologies for this. After all, managers have brought about a fundamental transformation in the way welfare organisations carry out government policy, as well as increasing their own power in the process (Clarke, 1998). As a result, what social workers now do is set and tightly controlled by managers. This change reflects a move away from the administration of public services to their management, a process that has been occurring since the 1970s (Harris and White, 2009a). It stemmed from the neoliberal ideology or belief that the market was superior to the state in every way and that public services needed to be managed in ways that were drawn from the private sector. Public sector professionals including social workers, the argument went, could no longer be protected and pampered by the administrative systems of the social democratic welfare state, and the view of service users as passive recipients of professional expertise also had to be challenged. Consequently, the extended role and increased power of managers, including their supposed ability to stand up for users against the assumed entrenched self-interest of professionals, was to undermine the administrative system that had provided the home and base within which welfare state professionalism had thrived.

Little has been made of the 'social work business' so far, but it is significant because it stems from the neoliberal view that public services, including social work, had to become more like businesses and operate in ways that were drawn from the private sector, thereby functioning in a context that was as market-like as possible (Harris, 2003). It meant that welfare state professionals including social workers needed to become engrossed in the bracing competitive stimulus of market forces, which necessitated managers rather than

---

professionals being the main instrument of effective social policy. One has only to witness the way managers and managerialism now dominate in the public services as a whole, whether it be education, health, the police or, of course, social work.

The increased influence of managers and managerialism and the development of the social work business occurred during the neoliberal Conservative governments of 1979–97. During that period, the Labour Party, which eventually became New Labour, increasingly echoed neoliberal themes and ideas by stressing the primacy of economic competitiveness, the subordination of social policy to the needs of a competitive national economy, the limited or reduced scope for government intervention or direction, and the need to control public expenditure (Harris and White, 2009a). As I have pointed out on numerous occasions, New Labour essentially accepted and endorsed Thatcherism's bequest of neoliberalism, and in so doing built on and extended this ideology into new areas.

In this chapter, I discuss these changes as they affected social work during the Thatcher/Major years, notably the emphasis on markets, the mixed economy and managerialisation, all of which anticipated much of the current situation. I then look in more detail at managerialism and the social work business. As a consequence of these developments, the prospects for meaningful social work, a practice that operates alongside users on the issues they face, looks rather bleak given the neoliberal world we now inhabit and which many struggle against.

Marketisation, the mixed economy and managerialisation

In an intriguing and prescient essay entitled 'After Social Work?', Clarke (1996) describes and discusses the changes associated with the neoliberal assault on welfare in general and social work in particular. He focuses on the social processes and forces that transformed social work in the 1980s and 1990s, all of which still have considerable influence. The crucial features of all this are marketisation, the mixed economy of welfare, and, importantly, what he terms 'managerialisation'.

Marketisation refers to the sponsored development of competition in the provision of welfare services together with the introduction of internal markets within public service organisations as a way of making them imitate market relationships. It is related to the moves towards contractual modes of relationship as a key feature of the organisation of service provision as well as the reduction of direct service provision by public institutions. Again the notion of 'quasi-markets' (Le Grand and Bartlett, 1993) is important, as it identifies the artificial, imitative and regulated nature of these marketised relationships, this being reflected in the distinct and peculiar position of the 'customer' in such markets. These market-making processes are linked to a mixed economy of welfare.

The mixed economy[1] is the sustained attempt to shift the balance of provision towards the independent sector of private and voluntary providers. Simultaneously direct provision through the welfare state becomes less central, resulting in the blurring of the boundaries between state and non-state welfare provision; activities previously performed by state agencies are contracted out, with private and voluntary agencies being brought into new relationships of partnership with the state, either by regulation or by dependence on it. Also included is the transferring of responsibilities from formal to informal provision, towards 'care by the community', which is essentially part of a wider privatisation of welfare responsibilities including health, education and income maintenance. It is not only older people or those with mental or physical health issues that have to increasingly rely on themselves or their family, and this means usually women, for care, but also troubled and troublesome young people, who are increasingly seen as the responsibility of parents and are offered only limited help and support. If this responsibility is not properly carried out, the interventions that do take place are more often than not punishment oriented. Examples of this include fining parents with young people who attend school irregularly, or making parents attend classes because of their children's offending. 'Devolving' such responsibilities to the family also redraws the public–private boundary and creates new forms of discipline and surveillance over family life (Donzelot, 1979).

The process of managerialisation has had a profound impact on social work and therefore, like Clarke (1996), I want to elaborate on this and, in particular, on two related aspects: first, the nature of modes of organisational coordination, which refers to the ways organisations are organised and interorganisational relationships are constructed; and second, the nature of organisational regimes including the patterns of structures, cultures and power within organisations. The point is that neither markets nor the mixed economy run themselves because they require agents to make them work, and over recent decades the preferred agents have been managers rather than professionals or administrators. This can be counterposed to bureau-professionalism, which is one label for the organisational regime of the social democratic welfare state where the dominant mode of coordination was rational administration and professional discretion (Newman and Clarke, 1994). This embodied the Fabian model of social welfare in that expertise could be applied to social problems and in so doing alleviate them. Modes of coordination included hierarchical authority and collegial relations, and featured claims to distinctive forms of neutrality in the form of bureaucratic rationality and professional knowledge and values.

Managerialisation, however, became the preferred mode of organisational coordination as a result of the economic, political and ideological changes associated with neoliberalism. These include the reconstruction of managerial power in the 1980s in a wider setting than had previously been the case and involved the reduction of trade union rights and powers together with the extension of managerial control over how to use workers. Such changes may have been pioneered in industrial settings, but they soon moved to the public services.

The rise in managerialisation can also be seen in terms of the particular definition of the crisis in the welfare state, which underpinned the managerial mode of coordination in the reconstruction of welfare. The neoliberal attack on welfare linked the fiscal crisis of welfare to a specific critique of the organisational patterns of welfare provision, namely Fabianism, associated with the social democratic consensus. Resonating with some earlier comments, this included attacks on 'provider power', such as bureaucratic rigidity, inflexibility, professional imperialism, insensitivity to users, lack of competition and the 'dogma' of political interference and control. All this provided the foundation for marketisation and changing the balance of the mixed economy, but in addition it supported the rise of managerial modes of coordination into public bodies as a precursor to reshaping their organisational regimes.

Although neoliberalism led to the rise of 'managerialisation' and the ensuing demise of Fabianism with its bureau-professional regimes, it is important to recall that such bureaucracies had many critics, ranging from those on the political left to feminists, minority ethnic groups and users. The point is, however, that neoliberals were in a position of power in the Conservative Party and were able to put their ideas into action. Furthermore, they were able to absorb many of these critiques, together with the space they created, and make them into a relatively systematic articulation that sought to speak for people against the power of the state or, more particularly, for the welfare 'customer' against the 'provider power' of the old regime (Clarke, 1994). This was the context in which managerialism gained prominence, something that continues to this day.

Managerialism

There are two key, interconnected, elements to managerialism (Lymbery, 2004a). First, as mentioned above, it aims to control bureau-professional power within organisations by subjecting them to new forms of regulation through centralised processes of financial control and methods of evaluation, as well as the increased power of the customer. Second, it involves recruiting organisations to processes of self-discipline characterised by the internalised acceptance of performance targets, increased bureaucracy and financial rationalisations and/or limits.

Since 1979, and increasingly over the past couple of decades, the concept of managerialism has been prevalent in the public services (Clarke and Newman, 1997; Harris, 2003; Evans, 2009). It is closely associated with the neoliberal critique of the idea of need that underpins professional practice and service provision in the welfare state. Needs are not things waiting to be identified by the competent observer, but are related to plans and purposes that are subjectively chosen; viewing needs as objective and distinct from wants, the argument continues, is paternalistic, which is what much of the activity of the welfare state actually is (Barry, 1999).

Another factor to consider is that 18 years of Conservative government resulted in social policy being increasingly based on a residual model of welfare. This reflected both an assumption that welfare is primarily the responsibility of the family and community, together with a belief that when the state intervenes it should provide only the basic minimum because welfare provided by the state is oppressive, inefficient and debilitating. Further, as we saw in Chapter Three, Hayek and Friedman argued that a lack of sensitivity to cost and a failure to be responsive to consumers in public services required the injection of market discipline to create efficiency, innovation and effective services. In addition, in contrast to Fabianism, they argued that the state's reliance on professionals and bureaucrats to decide people's needs and allocate support involved both a mistaken faith in professional expertise and an insupportable exercise of power over citizens. It is as a result of such arguments that managerialism became influential in two areas of the public services, namely health and social services.

This increasing influence is associated with two reports by Sir Roy Griffiths into health and social services (see Timmins, 1996). Interestingly, he was the head of Sainsbury's supermarkets when he did this work so what he actually knew about health and social services might well have been questioned, but that was not the concern of the Conservatives. It was what he knew about management and business that interested them. The government asked him to review 'manpower' and 'resources' within the NHS and community care services more generally. The first report (Griffiths, 1983) recommended a move away from a system of consensus management in which doctors played a powerful role in hospital management alongside administrators. Griffiths was concerned about the lack of clear lines of responsibility for management decision making and recommended establishing professional managers in place of administrators, giving them responsibility for budgetary control, monitoring performance and quality of service. The government's response was positive, resulting in managers, both from within and outside the NHS, being recruited. Management budgets and clear lines of financial accountability were also introduced. The second report (Griffiths, 1988) was driven by a concern to control rising central government expenditure on residential care through the benefits system. It recommended transferring government spending to local authorities, which should assess whether people needed public funding. Significantly, this negated the idea of social services or care as a universal service provided by the public sector. Instead such services were cast in the role of last resort, only to be contacted when the family or community were unable to provide support. The role of local authorities was to manage the market of care by coordinating services, both strategically and, in the form of care management, on an individual basis. The overall aim was to limit services within available resources. The report went on to recommend that local authorities should not be direct providers of services but instead make the best use of private and voluntary organisations so as to widen consumer choice, stimulate innovation and encourage efficiency.

The two Griffiths reports were significant in the advance of managerialism within health and social services, both being indicative of important issues about any critical analysis of managers and managerialism (Evans, 2009). The first promoted general management in the efficient running of the health service, while the second focused on structural change in terms of reducing public responsibility for social care. Importantly, however, managerialism has to be understood in terms of the relationship between organisational forms and a particular framework of values; it is not just a set of technical prescriptions of how to run an organisation, but includes assumptions about the relationship between the state and citizens/ customers, the role of public and private sectors, and the virtues of the market. It also conflates a desire for well-run public services with a neoliberal aversion to the nature and role of public provision of welfare. However, it goes without saying that managerialism is not alone in its concern for well-managed public services, nor in expressing concern about professionalism becoming a conspiracy against ordinary people. Going further though, a key criticism is the assumption that well-managed public services must act and look like business.

There is another issue to consider, namely that managerialism can involve different forms in different areas of public service, this being a reflection of the historical and organisational contexts of each service. Thus, the NHS and social services have different organisational contexts and challenges for managerialism because of the very different nature and role of managers in these services. Both have been targets for managerial reform because of the powerful role of professionals in these services, with some even seeing them as sites in which professionals have captured public organisations (see Harris, 2009), although this is truer of clinicians than social workers. In the NHS, managers, like the administrators before them, are a distinct professional group, differentiated from the clinicians they manage and largely recruited from the beginning into the administrator/manager role. In contrast, managers within social services were appointed from among the ranks of the professionals they managed. The different nature of these managers is evidenced by the fact that those in the NHS have extremely limited input into clinical decision making, whereas those in social services have historically had a strong role in case decision making. Consequently, the key point to note is that although managers may be similar in some ways, they can also be different in different contexts. Managerialism may well have common concerns and assumptions, but its focus and impact have to be understood within the specific contexts of operation.

As far as social services/care is concerned, the growth of managerialism occurred against the backdrop of bureau-professionalism, the combination of the organising principles of bureaucracy and professionalism in social services departments following their establishment in the wake of the Seebohm Report (1968). Such departments, while located in the bureaucratic structure of local authorities, were strongly influenced by professional principles of organisation whereby professional supervisors were supportive colleagues rather than directive managers. This included an emphasis on allowing professional staff, who were trusted by their fellow professionals occupying the significant senior posts within social services departments, a significant degree of discretion in their work (Clarke, 1996; Harris, 2003). Here managers were largely committed to the idea of professional social work and their rise in the organisational hierarchy was based on professional standing as well as managerial authority.

As Evans (2009) points out, social work's commitment to human rights and social justice may involve complex ideas and be open to different interpretations, but they do provide the fundamental milieu within which the 'value talk' of social work is generated and maintained. Within the context of bureau-professionalism, social work and social services expressed these commitments in terms of Marshall's (1996 [1950]) notion of social citizenship. This is the view that in order to achieve full and equal participation in society, all its members have the right to share in the complete social and cultural heritage, and to live the life of a civilised human being according to the standards prevailing in society. Furthermore, to realise this aim within the welfare state, professionals needed discretion not simply to implement policy but also to develop it by translating general welfare rights into particular provision. The advance of managerialism significantly challenged this view, resulting in major changes in the distribution and balance of power within social services and social work, including the displacement of traditional professional concern with needs, and social citizenship by business concerns of economy and efficiency in service delivery. It amounts to what might be termed the 'fiscalisation' of policy and practice, whereby policy and practice decisions are made on the basis of financial concerns rather than social and moral values.

Another way of looking at some of these issues is to see the modes of management and governance in public services as encouraging means to be separated from ends in organisational practices (see Green, 2009). 'Quasi-markets', 'competitive tendering', 'purchaser–provider splits', 'management by objectives' and so forth have all contributed to this development, a situation whereby process and compliance, rather than initiative and professional judgement, come to the fore. In our case, social workers are judged favourably by conforming to prescribed targets and their organisation's reputation is judged primarily on meeting similar pre-specified targets and performance indicators. The predominant values in the organisation have become the instrumental goals of demonstrating organisational success or 'getting things done efficiently and effectively', rather than meeting need, with social workers often having little option but to comply.

Domination or discursive mangerialism?

In the context of the advancement of managerialism, two broad strands can be discerned – the 'domination' and 'discursive' perspectives (Evans, 2009). In simple terms, the former sees managers and professionals as two distinct occupational groups: managers run organisations with their primary commitment being to the organisations' goals, while professionals and practitioners are the workers within the organisations. Managers are seen to have increased their power within social work and social services, are preoccupied with the organisation itself and are antithetical to practitioners' professional concerns. Their authority is simply based on hierarchical position that may or may not relate to their professional standing, and they enforce their authority by means of coercive strategies because practitioners are seen as self-interested workers who must be directed and monitored. They are involved in an endless struggle with practitioners and use a range of techniques such as procedures, performance indicators, and budget and eligibility criteria to exert control and achieve organisational goals. Their overriding concerns are controlling professional practice and enforcing organisational aims such as the rationing of resources (Howe, 1991; Jones 1999, 2004). The community care reforms of the early 1990s can be seen as a pivotal point in the shift of power and control from practitioners to managers, with the role of social workers becoming more prescribed and inflexible as a more prominent role was expected from their managers. The Conservative government of the time felt that frontline managers could simultaneously regulate the duties of social workers, oversee the stricter eligibility criteria for services applied to service users and thereby, overall, protect finite resources. Twenty years later, we now have the prime minister of the Conservative–Liberal Democratic coalition, David Cameron, arguing that public services need to 'do more for less', and this oft-repeated phrase would now surely not sound remiss coming from the lips of senior New Labour politicians.

The 'discursive' perspective offers perhaps a more optimistic view of the encroachment of the managerial tide. Here, there is not a distinct break from bureau-professionalism to managerialism, with instead a continuation of professional concerns and practices being able to operate, albeit in conjunction with an increasingly powerful managerial discourse. Drawing on aspects of Foucault and postmodernism more generally, the emphasis is on the fragmentary and dispersed nature of power, with the idea of dominance being problematic and the techniques of control more ambiguous than the domination perspective suggests. Managers are not simply seen as being engaged with and committed to a managerial discourse, and neither are practitioners necessarily its passive subjects or immune to it. They are not two distinct and homogeneous groups, but rather actors who operate within fields of crisscrossing forces. Consequently, managerialism has not replaced bureau-professionalism, but arguably is another organisational stratum laid on it that may be thick or thin, robust or weak, depending on particular times and in particular circumstances (Clarke and Newman, 1997). This discursive view sees organisational and management practices as being able to reflect professional strategies and concerns alongside increasingly influential managerialist ideas and preoccupations, and, in so doing, provide new focal points of resistance, compromise and accommodation.

Whatever the merits of the 'domination' and 'discursive' views, there are two important issues in relation to the advance of managerialism. First, social workers are undoubtedly now more subject to the control and direction of managers and, second, managers as a group are now by and large distinct from practitioners as far as their commitments and interests are concerned. There has been an increase in the proceduralisation of practice, with practitioners now subject to ever more intense direction and scrutiny (Jones, 2004; Lymbery, 2004a). Although some argue that resulting rules and procedures help ensure good practice and even support expertise, increased proceduralisation also reflects business principles. This is because the focus is increasingly on the economy, efficiency and effectiveness of the organisation itself, which in turn involves the need to control practitioners. Even if at times rules and procedures need interpretation and the application of some background knowledge, hence allowing an element of discretion, few would disagree with the proposition that generally they amount to an 'iron cage' that limits practitioner discretion. As for managers being a distinct group who have left behind their professional identity and have instead become more business-like by embracing business wisdom and concerned primarily with the organisation, there is certainly some evidence of this. For example, Harris (1998) shows that managers are encouraged to develop business skills and this tendency increased under New Labour. Then again, Clarke (2004) points out that there has been a concerted effort to shift what were professional identities to organisation-centred ones; the organisation becomes the point of identification, loyalty and commitment, with externally oriented identities, such as simply being a member of the British Association of Social Workers, being treated as suspect and as a 'special interest' that distracts from the organisation. Finally, one has only to recall that many senior managers in charge of social work do not have a social work qualification. Following the demise of social services departments, many of those who took over as heads or senior managers of the subsequent adults and children's services had no experience of social work, although they may have been qualified in, or have had experience of, business. Following the Baby Peter tragedy, the lack of many senior managers' social work experience was one of the many criticisms of London Borough of Haringey's children's services.

The social work business

John Harris (2003), in his seminal text *The Social Work Business*, shows how every aspect of social work has been deeply affected by the imposition of a culture of managerialism and competition, particularly over the past 15 years. One consequence of that culture is that a profound dissatisfaction now exists among social workers about what their jobs now entail, with a growing gap arising between their daily tasks and duties, and the values that brought them into the job in the first place (Jones, 2004). This has arisen largely because of 'modernisation', a crucial component of New Labour ideology that entails 'bringing individuals, communities and institutions, whether professional or governmental into line with the perceived requirements of a globalised world economy' (Ferguson, 2008, p 46). For social work, the creation of the 'social work business' was significant and involved the three elements – the 'universalisation of managerialism' (Clarke, 2004, p 121), regulation and consumerism – all of which are key in understanding the social work business.

The universalisation of managerialism

Effective management is seen as the panacea for practically every problem facing public services. Under the Conservatives, public service administrators were supposedly reinvented as dynamic individuals so as to overthrow bureaucratic and professional barriers to change and create a mixed economy of care in which the private sector is increasingly involved. As noted above, one consequence of this was that senior managers who were former social workers were gradually replaced by people with no social work qualification. But it was not just within the hierarchy of public sector organisations that such changes occurred. The 1990 NHS and Community Care Act and subsequent guidance identified assessment and care management as the core social work roles, whereby the care manager assesses need and coordinates packages of care in a world where 'purchasers' and 'providers' are no longer the same people or organisations. The rhetoric referred to 'empowerment', 'choice' and 'needs-led assessment', but the consequence of these developments was the creation of the social work business, and the subsequent effects on social work practice were to be far-reaching. As Harris (2003, p 66) points out, managerialism and the social work business took social work 'away from approaches that were therapeutic or which stressed the importance of casework, let alone anything more radical or progressive. Turning professionals into managers involved making them responsible for running the "business"'.

Developments in relation to the social work business continued and intensified under New Labour, with particular emphasis on the 'integration of services' so as to place the service user at the centre (Audit Commission, 2002). This is reflected in the establishment of various multi-agency structures over recent years. Then there was the demise of social services departments, which were split in two with, in essence, children's services merging with education, and adult services with health. There may well be benefits to health, education, social work and other professions working together, such as breaking down cultural barriers and more effective sharing of information. However, there is a danger that more powerful professions such as the police, health and education dominate at the expense of less esteemed and less well organised professions and agencies like social work and voluntary sector organisations. In addition, the loss of an organisational base coupled with a weak professional identity could lead to the virtual disappearance of professions such as social work, as was pointed out well over a decade ago (see Clarke, 1996).

The expansion and intensification of regulation

Although the Conservative governments of the 1990s were content to allow managers to bring about transformation in the public services including social work, as we saw in Chapter Four, New Labour was more interventionist. This included a decidedly centralist attitude to towards policy making, with responsibility for implementation being 'franchised' to semi-independent organisations that are nevertheless closely regulated and controlled from the centre (Harris, 2003). The General Social Care Council and the Social Care Institute for Excellence, regulating the workforce and social work's knowledge base respectively, are obvious examples. Then there is the role of Ofsted in relation to the merged children's social care and education services. The result of these and other similar organisational changes has been that 'processes of external review, audit, inspection, national standards, as well as performance indicators covering almost every area of work, are now common features of social work and social care' (Ferguson, 2008, p 48). Scourfield (2007, p 176), writing about residential care but with his comments being equally applicable to social work, puts it this way: 'New Labour clearly believes that, by using regimes of regulation and audit, it can control and work through markets to achieve the dual goals of producing better quality services for consumers whilst, at the same time, putting the service user at the heart of the decision making'. These developments have taken place despite the fact that New Labour's general approach to the regulation of business was regularly described, notably by Gordon Brown both as Chancellor of the Exchequer and Prime Minister, as 'light' or 'soft' touch. One has only to witness New Labour's attitude to the energy companies and the financial sector, notwithstanding the fact that such an approach to banking led to the credit crunch and recession of 2008-10. There are two separate, but related, reasons why the social work business was treated differently.

First, like their Conservative predecessors, New Labour had a neoliberal distrust of professions as being self-serving groupings and of social work in particular because of its failings in relation to child protection. Then there is the fact that social workers often ally themselves to those who depend on an increasingly residual welfare state, and are therefore seen to be encouraging dependency. Greater regulation is required because social workers themselves cannot be trusted to bring about the necessary changes and thereby engage in the modernisation project. This argument, however, fails to address the fundamental point that, to the extent that social work is 'failing', such failure is more likely to be related to the imposition of a quasi-business system that subordinates the needs of service users and the knowledge and skills of social workers to the demands of competition within the social care market.

The second reason for increased regulation also relates to mistrust, but of a different kind. Although New Labour sees markets and competition in social work and social care, as well as elsewhere, as offering the best guarantee of choice and quality, it makes a concession to traditional social democratic thought in that it deems some regulation necessary to ensure that markets are working efficiently and standards are maintained. Simply put, in order to create the 'performance management and audit culture', you need tools such as Best Value frameworks, national standards, audits, league tables and inspection (Webb, 2006). Despite this, the point has to be made that there is little evidence that all this regulation, together with the resulting 'naming and shaming', does actually lead to an improvement in services. Rather the converse is nearer the truth: organisations merely adapt to meet their performance targets even though this can lead to poorer services for service users (Harris, 2003). One has only to recall that in the Baby Peter case the London Borough of Haringey had received a favourable inspection report prior to the tragedy. This had relied on quantitative data, for example how many forms had been filled in within specified timescales, rather than on the underlying quality of service provision and practice. Realising that this would be Ofsted's focus, the borough no doubt prioritised its work accordingly. Another example that springs to mind relates to the two-stage initial and core assessment process in relation to children and families. On occasions the number and completion times of such assessments within one authority is compared to those in neighbouring authorities. Depending on the result of the comparison, this can lead to more or fewer core assessments having to be completed, not on the basis of complexity, user circumstances or need but because of the necessity to be seen in a favourable light in relation to other authorities. A similar point could be made in relation to the numbers of contacts and subsequent referrals that are received; whether or not a contact becomes a referral often depends not on user circumstance or need, but on a comparison with figures from neighbouring authorities and even a comparison with teams within the same authority. Similarly, whether a home visit following a referral remains just that or necessitates an initial assessment can again depend on comparing figures rather than the presenting situation and the overall facts and circumstances of the particular case.

Webb (2006) points out two other consequences of this 'performance culture'. First, the social work role is increasingly conceived of, and limited to, gatekeeping and the rationing of resources, so that the focus is on higher-level assessment and planning. Little remains of preventative social work, this being the remit of standardised assessment tools such as the Common Assessment Framework, which 'anyone can do'. Even higher-level assessment and planning is dominated by standardised assessment forms and computer exemplars that contribute to the deprofessionalisation of social work. Second, such a culture changes the relationship between social workers and service users, with the former increasingly concerned about managing budgets and reducing risk. As many social workers have repeatedly pointed out, they often spend more time dealing with budgets and paperwork than they do meeting the real needs of people (Jones, 2004).

Consumerism and the 'business'

Consumerism, is a major aspect of the social work business. It is frequently linked to 'user involvement' or 'user empowerment', with two models discernable though often conflated in theory and practice (Beresford and Croft, 1993, 1995). The first is the consumerist model of user involvement enshrined in the 1990 NHS and Community Care Act and subsequent guidance. Although it aimed to empower users and carers, it also provided the statutory basis for the greater involvement of the private sector in social care. The second model is concerned with people, not primarily in terms of their relationship with services but rather as citizens who may also make use of health and social care services because of difficulties associated with physical impairment, mental distress or age. It is often referred to as the 'democratic' model of user/citizen empowerment and differs from consumerist models in that it is a 'bottom up' approach emerging from collective movements; it is aimed at social change and justice rather than just involvement in services; it has a social ideology rather than an individual or biomedical model of health and disability; and it often involves collective action rather than mere partnership with service providers. The interaction between these models means 'the experience of social work and social services for many service users may be the same or even worse than twenty or thirty years ago.... At the same time, there are examples of change that could not have been conceived of in the recent past' (Beresford and Croft, 2004, p 63).

Even though he is best known as a critic of marketisation, Harris (2004) points to three areas where consumerist approaches have assisted in social development. First, the ambiguity of the language of consumerism and its accurate identification of the lack of user involvement in traditional welfare services have actually encouraged users and carers to become more involved. Second, consumerism's (de)construction of the client/user as 'customer' has led to an emphasis on procedural rights, such as the right to a needs-led assessment, and new forms of redress by complaints procedures. These developments go some way to addressing the detail of the individual experience of the user. Third, the consumerist approach allows for more attention to individual needs based on individualised assessment rather than the 'one size fits all' approach.

There is no doubt that users and carers have become more involved in health and social care and some examples of this can be found in relation to government policy and legislation, service development, research and social work education (see Ferguson, 2008, pp 73-4) . For example, universities offering social work degrees must provide evidence of involving users and carers, for example in the planning of courses and in their selection, teaching and assessment of students. The development of procedural rights is also to be welcomed; surely no-one would disagree that those who use, or are forced to rely on, state-provided services should at least have basic procedural rights such as complaints procedures. However, the point about consumerist approaches leading to assessments and services tailored to individual need requires some qualification. Whatever empowering potential such assessments might have had, they were almost immediately constrained by the fact that soon after the 1990 Act was passed local authorities were allowed to take resource considerations into account when assessing individual needs. It is easy to make the point that such individualised assessments were less about need and more about the rationing of resources. Some 20 years later, such constraints are likely to have increased further. A similar comment about rationing can be made in relation to children's services' initial and core assessments. Unless there are child protection/safeguarding concerns, social workers are under pressure to offer little, if anything, other than at best, to offer advice or make a referral to the increasing number of agencies and voluntary organisations that deal with the various issues confronting children and families. Failing this, the continuation of universal services in the form of health and education is all that is required. It is surely no surprise that families are often likely to feel that their issues and concerns are not being taken seriously by social workers and that they are being 'fobbed off'.

Direct payments (DPs) are another area that has been transformed by marketisation, together with associated notions of consumerism and the 'business'. DPs were introduced in the 1990s for people with disabilities; social services departments gave money directly to individuals to buy the support they had been assessed as needing instead of providing the services themselves. Spandler (2004) asks whether such payments are 'friend' or foe'? In fact there are two arguments for saying they are empowering. First, they sit well with New Labour's notions of choice, flexibility and the user as customer. Second, disability activists have campaigned for them for some time, seeing DPs as a means of disabled people gaining greater control of their own lives. Given the history of paternalist, sometimes oppressive and even abusive institutionalisation service provision, the attractions of DPs are easy to see. They appear to offer an element of choice, control, flexibility and independence, and the focus on choice and control, rather than illness or disability, means they can be seen as embodying a social, rather than medical, model of health and disability (Beresford and Croft, 2004). They also offer a pointer as to how services could be organised differently so as to reflect the needs and wishes of those who depend on them.

But despite the apparent positives, there are concerns. First, they were introduced in the context of the social work business, the overriding objective being to reduce public spending and to extend market forces into all areas of health and social care. This means that although in principle there is no set financial limit on the size of DPs, in practice they are constrained by the state of local authority budgets. There is evidence that local authorities have seen DPs as a means of saving money, even to the extent that cost cutting has been one of the main attractions of DPs (Spandler, 2004).

Second is the complexity of managing and administering a payment through the DP scheme. This can involve the recipient having to open a dedicated bank account, which in itself is not always straightforward for those living in disadvantaged areas. Then there is the clerical and administrative burden of having to submit monthly statements and returns. Another factor is the problems associated with the user taking on the responsibilities of an employer, including recruiting (and dismissing) personal assistants. Middle-class service users who have business, managerial, supervisory or similar backgrounds may find such issues easier to deal with, but this is not necessarily the case for those without such advantages. In this scenario, the question arises as to whether DPs maintain or widen inequalities.

Third, collective service provision can be undermined by the individualisation of service provision that DPs involve. Spandler (2004), referring to the situation in Canada where a similar system has been in place for much longer than in the UK, notes that it is a real threat to a healthy and vibrant public sector where best practice and standards are collectively developed.

The final concern relates to the implications of DP schemes for those who provide the care. Consistent with the culture of consumerism, care users and givers are largely left to their own devices, not least in terms of how the former recruits and organises their care. They operate in a labour market based on low wages and few skills and qualifications, where the organisation of personal assistants (PAs) is virtually non-existent (Ungerson, 2004). A possible positive aspect of this situation is that users can control who provides the care and the type of care provided, but the negative aspect relates to the fact that some may feel they can call on workers outside their contractual hours and even without payment, thus making such workers vulnerable to exploitation. This also leads to the question of who would want to be such a worker, given the low pay, unsocial hours and lack of training (Scourfield, 2005). The answer is likely to be those with no other options, so there is no real surprise that finding PAs is a problem for service users, either because they are unsuitable or because there is too much competition from other providers or simply insufficient numbers of applicants. It should also be noted that those who do apply are exempt from the scope of the General Social Care Council's registration of people working in social care, and that users cannot access the Criminal Records Bureau to check potential applicants' backgrounds. The increased potential for service user abuse within such an unregulated market is plain to see. At the very least, and as with all New Labour 'transformation' and 'modernisation' agendas, surely the transformative power of DPs should be questioned.

The most recent development of consumerism in relation to social work and social care is personalisation. This has been dealt with in Chapter Four so I will not dwell on it here other than to make two points. First, to reiterate some earlier comments, personalisation is essentially about ensuring that people take more responsibility for the services they receive, that they become the 'choosing', 'deciding' and 'shaping' authors of their own lives by assessing and managing their own health and welfare. Although this may be a superficially attractive scenario, it fails to acknowledge the combination of poverty, multiple discrimination, and, often, physical or mental impairment experienced by many users of social work and social care. Proponents ignore the impact of structural inequality, the results of which were repeatedly pointed out by the late sociologist and social justice campaigner Professor Peter Townsend. Furthermore, the fact that all the political parties are intent on reducing expenditure on every aspect of public services including social care means such policy changes are likely to be experienced as punitive rather than empowering.

The second point relates to the effect personalisation is likely to have on social workers. Some local authorities are planning to cut qualified social worker posts while increasing the number of non-qualified workers to implement the reforms (Rogowski, 2009). The concern is the systematic deskilling of social work in this area, whereby professional judgement is sacrificed on the altar of choice and control. The real danger is that the introduction of personalisation will lead to the creation of unqualified bureaucrats who, it is worth repeating, will be cheaper to employ, as well as being easier to manage and control. They will, therefore, be more willing and able to tick choice-denying boxes rather than support users to achieve the best quality of life open to them, even if it is more expensive for the public purse.

Having looked at how the social work business has changed social work, how has the 'business' and the emphasis on the market changed social care more generally, particularly in relation to privatisation issues and the increased involvement of the voluntary sector?

Social care: privatisation and the voluntary sector

First there is a need for a little history. The introduction of a business culture that included the profit motive into the domain of health and social care during the 1980s and 1990s could well have provoked public opposition, so phrases like the 'mixed economy of care' and 'empowerment of service users and carers' as well as the 'independent sector' were deliberately obscure and misleading. In particular, the 'independent sector' was a new term that embraced both commercial and voluntary organisations, collapsing some previous distinctions between them and cloaking the profit motive with the use of the private sector in social services/care provision (Harris, 2003). From this situation, it is not totally surprising that the management style and ethos of voluntary organisations were to change, and, following Ferguson (2008), questions arise as to whether the introduction of competition between providers has led to more choice, quality, independence and empowerment for service users, or whether services and staff conditions have suffered in the requirement to secure contacts.

Until the 1980s, the private sector only played a limited role in the provision of social care because of ideological and financial reasons. Until the arrival of neoliberalism, there was virtual unanimous agreement that the profit motive should not come into play when it came to meeting people's basic health and social care needs. In any case, the dominance of local authority provision plus the fact that most people who required it only had limited incomes meant it was an area that did not attract profitable investment. Two factors are relevant in understanding how the situation changed. First, there was a growth in private sector residential provision as a result of changes in the social security system that meant that the board and lodging costs of older people with assets under £3,000 were paid by the state. Second, there was the second Griffiths (1988) report into community care, which recommended the private sector be stimulated and encouraged. The result was that by the end of the 1990s, local authority provision of care had decreased and there was a corresponding increase in the independent sector provision. Similar changes took place in relation to domiciliary care provision over the same period, with the private sector playing an increasing role. In children's services, comparable measures occurred in relation to the growth of private children's homes particularly during the New Labour years. The current situation can be summarised as successive governments encouraging the marketisation and privatisation of residential and other forms of care, resulting in the 'caretelisation' of care as large corporate providers continue to increase their share of the market (Scourfield, 2007).

Perhaps the rapid growth in the private sector provision of social care would not be a problem if it could be shown that it had led to improvements in the quality of life of those using residential or home care services. However, the reverse seems to be the case (Pollock, 2004). In the first place, the large-scale provision of private residential care detracts from the quality of care and contributes to a sense of institutionalisation. Put simply, economies of scale mean that larger homes with more beds make more profit. Then there is the fact that the emphasis on profit means there is a constant need to drive down costs, with obvious implications for staff wages, workload and training, and in turn the overall quality of care. Bardsley (2009, p 32) draws on her experience of over 20 years as a home help/support worker to argue that 'standards of service undoubtedly suffered as profit driven private companies sought to lower their wage bills, make people work harder and failed to take training seriously'. She also points to how visits to users were rushed and sometimes did not even take place because of the pressure of the work. Furthermore, users often did not even know who was coming to visit them, causing considerable confusion, upset and distress.

In some cases, failure to make a profit means homes may have to close, with elderly and vulnerable residents having to leave what may have been their home for years. Marketisation and privatisation processes not only mean that public accountability is diminished, but also that principles such as consumer choice and user involvement are likely to be compromised by allowing social care to be dictated by market forces. At the very least, the wisdom and morality of placing vulnerable people, of whatever age, in homes run by companies whose prime responsibility is to their shareholders needs to be questioned.

As well as the expansion of the private sector into social care, there has been even greater involvement of the voluntary (or third) sector. On one level, this may be less objectionable than the growth of the private sector, but 'in reality the same ideological, legislative and policy drivers are in operation in both spheres' (Ferguson, 2008, p 59-60). This involvement includes outsourcing local authority services, establishing market/quasi-market mechanisms and moving from unspecific grant to contract as the basis of funding. All were significant elements of the 1990 NHS and Community Care Act. The result is that voluntary sector organisations increasingly act like businesses and compete for contracts with the private sector; to all intents and purposes, they have become the 'soft face' of privatisation.

Under New Labour these processes continued and intensified, with the consequent different role of the sector having three profound consequences for the voluntary organisations themselves and for the people who use their services (Ferguson, 2008). First, there is increasing differentiation or inequality within the sector, as a tiny proportion of voluntary organisations receive by far the most government funding. An obvious problem here is that the smaller organisations often struggle to survive. Second, there is increasing differentiation and inequality within organisations; the pay and conditions of executives and managers far exceeds that of the majority of staff. And third, the move from unspecific grant to contract means the reciprocal relationship between local authority social services/care and the voluntary sector has been converted to a relationship based on exchange (Harris, 2003). Voluntary sector organisations become increasingly less concerned with finding solutions to local problems, and more concerned with competing for contracts to deliver centrally devised programmes. Their chief concern becomes one of service delivery agents who are trying to achieve target-driven government priorities. Other concerns relate to the dominance of short-term funding, the adequacy of funding and the fact that dependence on government contracts results in a reduced ability to act as advocates for their users (Charities Commission, 2007). It is not hard to see that the funding of organisations whose objectives are perceived as politically suspect or are not priorities will be under threat.

Conclusion

The market-driven agenda in relation to social work and social care more generally undoubtedly intensified under New Labour.

Although the party might be an amalgam of ideologies and discourses, (Powell, 1999), one must not forget that at its heart lies the neoliberal influence, hence the managerial and social work business culture that now dominates.

Social workers, at the behest of managers, are faced with a performance-, inspection- and target-driven culture that places huge pressure on them to achieve the desired paper and electronic outcomes. Various management tools including forms and templates aim to improve professional judgement by standardising responses and limiting the possibility of error. This reflects an adherence to scientific or instrumental rationalism, whereby the tools appear to hold out the promise of greater reliability by establishing systematic, objective and uniform practices. However, a practice standardised in this way has a one-sided focus on the bureaucratic elements, neglecting the ways that practitioners operationalise procedure. It pays little attention to the ways in which informal rationalities and methods, carried out within the context of a relationship, combine to make up practice, and it also pays little attention to the real needs of users.

The pressure on social workers is exerted by managers who face similar demands to satisfy their political masters. The stress is on encouraging the free market and limiting public expenditure, with budgetary considerations dominating decision making, meaning that genuinely meeting the real needs of users becomes a secondary consideration.

The move to the managerial and social work business is anathema to social work values and its commitment to social justice and social change. It is no wonder that social workers often feel disillusioned and demoralised by what has happened. Despite such pessimism, there are positive voices, ones that continue to see the progressive as well as the radical and critical possibilities. It is to these views, that I turn in the concluding chapter.

Note

[1] Actually Clarke (1996) refers to 'economies' rather than the conventional singular 'economy', arguing that there are multiple mixed economies with variations for different aspects of welfare and local rather than national formations. If for nothing else than convenience, however, I adhere to the singular.

SEVEN

Conclusion: the changing face or the fall of social work?

> The social work profession promotes social change, problem solving in human relationships and the empowerment of and liberation of people to enhance well being. Utilising theories of human behaviour and social systems, social work intervenes at the points where people interact with their environments. Principles of human rights and social justice are fundamental to social work. (IFSW, 2000)

The definition of social work by the International Federation of Social Workers (IFSW) reflects the day-to-day practice of most social workers, even if it is not always acknowledged. It goes on to refer to interventions ranging from psycho-social processes to involvement in social policy, planning and development. These include counselling, clinical social work, group work, family therapy and helping people obtain services and resources in the community. Also included are agency administration, community organisation and social/political action that has an impact on social policy and economic development.

However, there are two points to emphasise in relation to this definition. First, while administration warrants a mention, managerialism is conspicuous by its absence, despite the fact that it currently dominates social work in the UK. The second, linked, point is that following the changes arising from the neoliberalism of the past 30 years, many of the methods of intervention referred to are simply no longer used by British social workers (Horner, 2009). This is because 'in the broadest sense, the purposes [and the practices] of social work are determined by prevailing political ideologies' (Howe, 2002, p 86). As we are currently living in neoliberal times, this has had a negative impact on social work, and perhaps casts doubt on its ability to survive. To summarise, in many instances social workers have 'been turned into unreflective people-processors by waves of managerialism over the last 30 years and, more recently, by the intertwining of managerialism with New Labour's modernisation agenda' (White, 2009, p 129).

As we have seen, neoliberalism's concern with marketisation and reducing public expenditure has seen the introduction of managerialism to control financial costs and in turn social workers. If any intervention occurs, it is supposed to be evidence-based rather than a reflection of professional preference or opinion. In most cases, however, unless there are child protection/safeguarding concerns or a serious risk to oneself or others, little is offered in the way of intervention. Interventions that do occur are usually of a controlling, authoritarian nature, amounting to service users being told to change their lifestyles or face the consequences, which could mean either losing their children or their liberty.

Despite this, there are those from a critical perspective who manage to retain a sense of optimism concerning the future. It is to the recent work of three of these thinkers that I now turn: Garrett (2003, 2009b) on the remaking or transforming of social work with children and families; Ferguson (2008; Ferguson and Woodward, 2009) in relation to reclaiming social work together with reasserting a radical/critical approach; and Jordan (2007, 2008, 2010) on social work and well-being. The key question is that while the face of social work has undoubtedly changed, have we in effect witnessed its fall as a profession?

Remaking and transforming social work

Paul Michael Garrett (2003; 2009b) provides a sustained, critical account of the changes afflicting social work with children and families as a result of the neoliberal rationality that now dominates. These changes may have affected social work in many negative ways, but he argues that all is not necessarily lost. Drawing on Wade (2008), he also makes the point that the non-communist world has seen two shifts in international economic norms and rules separated by approximately 30 years. The first resulted in the social democratic era of the initial postwar years, which was characterised by Keynesianism and lasted until the mid-1970s. The second, neoliberalism, followed and was centred on notions that all governments should liberalise, privatise and deregulate. The most serious crisis of capitalism since 1929–33 began in 2008 and has led to suggestions that a further economic regime change is under way. If this is the case, it might lead to a more positive future for social work itself.

In looking at 'neoliberal transformation' and its impact on social work, things certainly look unpromising, as we have seen throughout this book. But if one returns to theorising neoliberalism more generally, some positive points emerge. This is because neoliberalism, although the dominant 'common sense' or ideology, does contain flaws and inconsistencies. In the first place, while the role of the state is to produce conditions conducive to neoliberalism, as Bourdieu (2001) reminds us it is not just simply something that is in the hands of the ruling class. The neoliberal state is complex and, at times, contradictory, thereby including spaces for potential opposition. It may not be completely neutral or completely independent of the dominant sources of power in society, but the more advanced it is, and the greater the social advances it has incorporated, the more autonomous it can be.

Then there is the fact that there is a disjuncture between neoliberalism, which exists at the theoretical level or as a system of thought, and day-to-day realities (Brenner and Theodore, 2002). For instance, there is a disjuncture between the ideology of neoliberalism – a utopia of free markets without state interference – and its practical political operation and effects, which have seen an intensification of state interference so as to impose market rules in all areas of social life. In addition, whereas neoliberal ideology entails that self-regulating markets provide the best allocation of investments and resources, neoliberal political practice has resulted in market failures (the banking crisis, resulting credit crunch and worlwide recession is an obvious example), new forms of market polarisation and an intensification of uneven development. One factor to consider is that neoliberals often do not have a blank canvas on which to operate and so falter because they must engage with ingrained cultures that, because they are not in tune with neoliberal 'common sense', generate resistance. Social workers, along with practitioners in a range of other professional fields, often have a loyalty to the practices and norms of their discipline as well as what amounts to the imposed practices and norms of the market. The resulting tension between a value base reflected in a humanistic code of ethics and one based on the market can lead to opposition to the privatisation of services, together with the development of counter-strategies to 'modernisation'.

Garrett (2009b), following Bourdieu (for example, 2001; Bourdieu et al, 2002) and Gramsci (see, for example, Joseph, 2006; Robinson, 2006), goes on to show how winning 'hearts and minds' is part of the neoliberal project. It is useful to dwell on this a little here, simply because of the lack of hope currently felt by many social workers.

The main political and social struggle of the present is that against the scourge of neoliberalism, notwithstanding the difficulties arising from the discursive formulation that disguises the true intent of the project. At least two points are worth emphasising here. First, there has been a massive redistribution of wealth in favour of the rich over the past 30 years. Vast transfers occurred in Russia following the demise of the USSR in the 1990s, and similar, if less extreme, developments have occurred in the UK and US. Importantly, these regressive changes have reversed the positive trends that occurred in the latter two countries during the social democratic era. The second, related, point is that many people are experiencing feelings of insecurity and general precariousness (Young, 2007), not just in relation to their working lives but also in relation to health, education and welfare services more generally. The fact is that when taxation was more progressive, it helped fund a robust welfare state that since the mid-1970s has increasingly been dismissed as a failed experiment that encouraged dependency and was unaffordable. This is despite the fact that such welfare services really did make a real and lasting difference to peoples' lives irrespective of their wealth. Since then, various neoliberal governments have increasingly encouraged, even pressurised, individuals to become more responsible for themselves and their families in all aspects of their lives. Simultaneously, rather than ensuring that all hospitals and schools are of a good standard, successive neoliberal governments have, through the introduction of various targets and performance indicators, forced these organisations or 'businesses' to compete with each other to survive. Individuals, or 'consumers' and 'customers' as they now tend to be referred to, face increasingly intrusive questions and often coercive measures in order to obtain the services or benefits they are entitled to. This certainly often applies to those who approach social workers for help or advice.

A conservative revolution

One of the principal features of *'conservative revolutions'* (Bourdieu, 2001, p 35, emphasis in original) is that they present restorations as revolutions, something 'new', 'modern' and amounting to 'modernisation'. The current revolution sanctions and exalts the reign of financial markets in this way, although, perversely, they serve no other law than to make maximum profit regardless of the costs to fellow human beings. The esteem in which financial markets are held also fails to acknowledge the inherent dangers of unbridled selfishness and greed that have led to the current global recession. Instead of a narrow and short-term concern with economics itself, there should be far more emphasis on the 'economics of happiness' (Bourdieu, 2001, p 40), something I return to through Bill Jordan's work. Bourdieu (2001, p 37) is also aghast at the dismantling of the 'economic and social bases of the most precious gains of humanity [not least the welfare state]' and also queries what he sees as essentially the falsehood of globalisation, which is often merely rhetoric invoked by governments in order to justify their surrender to financial markets. Many intellectuals and trade unions oppose this rhetoric, and I would include in this group green/environmental, feminist and anti-racist campaigners (Leonard, 1997), all of whom have formed alliances in the anti-globalisation/capitalist protests of recent years. What they all have in common is seeing the possibility of a more just and equal world.

Turning more specifically to social work, a similar optimism can be found, even if it has to be acknowledged that many social workers feel abandoned, disowned, even disillusioned and demoralised, by having to deal with the 'material and moral suffering that is the only certain consequence' of neoliberalism (Bourdieu et al, 2002, p

183). More positively, however, there is an important contradiction and with this some hope. This contradiction is that the 'initiative, the inventiveness, if not charisma of those functionaries [social workers] who are the least imprisoned in their function' is the only way that their bureaucracies can actually function, because otherwise the bureaucracy would in effect silt up and become paralysed. Moreover, this contradiction opens up a space where freedom and initiative can be used for the benefit of users and to 'defend the bureaucracy itself' (Bourdieu et al, 2002, p 191).

Seeing 'modernisation' as 'conservative revolution' shows how the struggle against neoliberalism involves a struggle over meaning, with Gramsci's notion of 'hegemony' being of particular relevance. 'Hegemony' implies the active and practical involvement of the hegemonised groups, which can be contrasted with the dominant ideology concept that is arguably more about a more static and passive subordination (Joseph, 2006). Consequently, for a hegemonic project to work it has to address and respond to people's lived experience of the world. In relation to children's services, for example, as Garrett (2009b) shows, appeals have to be made to professional values and intuitions in order to win over people who might have doubts and anxieties about 'modernisation'(see, for example, Chapter Four in relation to social work practices). Consequently, Gramsci was keen to stress how rule or dominance is something that is constructed rather than merely given. This requires us to consider various and potentially opposed future projects, even if there are dominant voices and forces (Clarke, 2004). Attention has also to be given to words in that there are key words and phrases that can, often without being noticed, contribute to the neoliberal hegemonic order. 'Modernisation', 'transformation' and 'flexibility' are obvious examples, but there are other more welfare-oriented words and phrases, such as 'problem families', 'the underclass', 'social exclusion', 'welfare dependency', 'consumer' and 'customer', all of which should be investigated and contested.

Despite the emphasis on words and discursive struggle, it has to be said that Gramsci acknowledged the need for a more orthodox politics based on political parties, trade unions, professional associations and social groups in which it is possible to create counter-hegemonic strategies aimed at social change.

An opening up of progressive possibilities

Having considered some of the ways to stem the rising tide of neoliberalism, albeit at a mainly abstract or theoretical level, Garrett (2009a) indicates how the Baby Peter case at the London Borough of Haringey opened up spaces for a more progressive debate about the 'transformation' of children's services and social work for children and families. The Baby Peter tragedy occurred against a policy background influenced by *Every Child Matters* (DfES, 2004) and the 2004 Children Act, both of which reflected New Labour's project to transform children's services (again, see Chapter Four). The range of policy initiatives that followed influenced the way social work for this user group has been organised and provided, reflecting the 'transformational reform agenda' (DfES, 2006, p 2). Significantly, however, many social workers are wary, even distrustful, about the direction of the 'reforms'. One of the messages to come out of two conferences held in 2006 (one of which I attended and referred to in Chapter One) was 'that many practitioners felt under threat from a New Labour administration seemingly tough on social work and tough on the values of social work' (Garrett, 2009a, p 534). Then again, the Audit Commission (2008, p 1) reported that children's trusts, the successors to social services departments, were 'confused and confusing' with 'little evidence of better outcomes for children and young people'. Although professionals were 'working together', no doubt much like they always had, this was 'often through informal arrangements outside the trust framework'. Trusts were found to 'get in the way' of this, and their overall 'purpose [was] 'unclear'.

In 2008, the political and media furore over Baby Peter began in earnest, even on occasions displacing coverage of the growing economic crisis. One could argue that the Baby Peter case, with its easily identifiable 'evil-doers', was some sort of distraction from the new, unfolding politics of insecurity and anxiety instigated by the ever-deepening economic recession. And if one looks at the main themes of the media frenzy, a 'largely retrogressive politics' (Garrett, 2009a, p 536) can be discerned.

First there was the targeting and vilification of individual public service professionals for failing to protect the child, which was similar to what occurred in the earlier Victoria Climbié case. Threats were even made to some individuals, fuelled by the media's increasingly hostile coverage. Second, much of the language used can be seen as part of the regulatory social agenda of neoliberalism. The partner of Baby Peter's mother was often described as 'evil' and although he may have possessed such a characteristic, simply dwelling on this notion was a far from adequate explanation of what occurred. So, too, was linking the tragedy to 'problem families', 'neighbours from hell' or 'the underclass'. Such media commentary perhaps has more to do with an element of 'class loathing and contempt' than any serious attempt to address the issues raised by the case (Garrett, 2009a, p 538). Similarly, the tendency to link the Baby Peter tragedy to a wider societal crisis, or 'broken society', as reflected in comments by senior Conservatives including the now prime minister, David Cameron, is an inadequate response. Nevertheless, this theme was given added impetus by David Cameron following the Edlington child torture case[1].

It was left to the joint area review (JAR) of Haringey Children's Services (Ofsted, Healthcare Commission, HM Inspectorate of Constabulary, 2008) to be the first to open up some space for more progressive debates on the 'transformation' agenda. The review pointed out that services were inadequate and required improvement, although this raised a number of significant issues.

As noted in the previous chapter, attention was focused on Ofsted itself, which had previously approved of services in Haringey. The review pointed out that there had been too much reliance on quantitative data and not enough on the underlying quality of service provision and practice. Second, the review increased public awareness about the electronic recording system social workers were forced to use, one result of this being that cases can be allocated without any prior discussion, and another being the amount of time social workers spent sat in front of computers (Hall et al, 2008). Third, there was a more sensible debate about what could and could not be achieved by social workers, namely that although generally the child protection/safeguarding system works well (Smith, 2004; Pritchard and Williams, 2010), risk and child deaths cannot be *totally* eliminated. Unlike the private sector, which can inflate product claims, social workers, together with others in the public sector, generally cannot and do not. Fourth, attention was focused on how neoliberal policies, reflected in unfilled vacancies, agency staff and high staff turnover, were affecting social workers' ability to deliver effective services (Unison, 2009).

Many of the points raised by the JAR report were echoed in the subsequent Social Work Task Force report (2009). As we saw in Chapter Five, the task force was established in the wake of the Baby Peter tragedy and focused on the recruitment, training and overall quality and status of social work in England. All three major political parties accepted the recommendations, but following David Cameron's (narrow) general election success in May 2010 and the announcement that there would be massive expenditure cuts, one has to seriously wonder whether the recommendations will see the light of day. Despite this, it really did seem that the Baby Peter case had opened up a space for debate about New Labour's 'modernisation' and 'transformation' agenda, and again this is something to which I will return.

Reclaiming social work

In many ways, Iain Ferguson (2008; Ferguson and Woodward, 2009) has similar concerns to Garrett when it comes to the dominance of neoliberalism, how it has changed social work and why the profession should be reclaimed. Similarly, the British Association of Social Workers (BASW) seemed to waken from its slumbers in 2009, organising conferences and a rally in London on the theme of 'taking back' the profession. During 2010, BASW has also been active in trying to ensure the establishment of a college for social work that is independent from government.

Various criticisms of neoliberalism have been discussed in this book, but perhaps the main one is that despite its claim that wealth trickles down to everyone, it actually leads to greater inequality.

Again, one has only to note that under the Thatcher and Major governments not only did inequality grow, but there also was an actual redistribution of wealth from the poor to the rich. As a result, New Labour inherited 'levels of poverty and inequality unprecedented in post-war history' (Hills and Stewart, 2005, p 1). Poverty is of vital significance to social workers because of the simple fact that most of the people they deal with are poor. Under New Labour, with 'welfare to work' rather than redistribution of wealth being seen as the answer, poverty continued to be a significant problem; even child poverty, the eradication of which had been a key policy target, remained stubbornly high. Tackling inequality ceased to be a Labour priority, so the gap between rich and poor continued and intensified. Contrary to what many New Labour politicians may think, however, inequality does matter, whether on moral grounds because it is incompatible with social justice, because of its correlation with other forms of inequality such as health, or merely because inequality can be linked to the exploitation of others.

As stated previously, another consequence of the dominance of neoliberalism is the creation of a society in which people feel insecure. Beck (1992) sees this as the 'risk society', whereby risks are now the by-products of developments in science and technology that affect *everyone*. Global warming is a prime example of one such risk. This can be counterposed to the risks associated with the 'industrial society', which were linked to class, poverty and inequality. Beck argues that the management of risk has replaced accumulation as the dynamic of neoliberal society. But surely risk, either environmental or social in relation to employment, health, education and welfare more generally, is a secondary consideration for those whose main concern continues to be the accumulation of wealth. Moreover, a key point often ignored is that while everyone may be at risk, some are at greater risk than others. Wealthy people can take steps to ensure that they are less affected by global warming, and they are also less affected by social risks, by, for example, being able to 'choose' which schools their children go to simply by moving house. Meanwhile, those without wealth face a precarious future in an increasingly privatised world. Ironically, given New Labour's emphasis on 'putting children first' or 'every child mattering', it is children who are at greatest risk of insecurities (UNICEF, 2007). Interestingly, two of the leading countries of the neoliberal experiment, the US and UK, have some of the most unhappy children in the world, anxious and fearful of the future and often involved in drug or alcohol misuse and crime.

Ferguson (2008; Ferguson and Woodward, 2009) also takes serious issue with developments affecting social work as a result of neoliberal policies, not least managerialism, competition and marketisation. The bureaucracy associated with completing forms as quickly as possible so as to meet targets, and with acting as care managers, rationers of resources and, increasingly, 'moral police', all contribute to a profound sense of dissatisfaction among social workers. It is not surprising that they are disillusioned about what their job has become and the increasing discrepancy between the reality of their day-to-day tasks and the values that brought them into the job in the first place. It amounts to the frustration of 'hopes, beliefs and desires by ideologies and policies which insist that the primary role of social workers is to "manage" "high-risk" families or individuals, to ration increasingly meagre resources, and collude in the demonization of groups such as young people and asylum seekers' (Ferguson, 2008, p 4). However, with this dissatisfaction the seeds of resistance are sown, and not only in those relatively small numbers of radical or critical social workers. Because managerialism and its associated developments undermine *all* forms of social work practice, dissatisfaction and resistance has potentially spread that much further so as to embrace a larger number of workers. It is also fuelled and strengthened by the emergence of two types of social movements, namely the social welfare and anti-globalisation/capitalist movements. Social welfare movements around disability and mental health issues have challenged traditional models of social work and ways of delivering services while also being at the forefront of resisting attempts to reduce welfare spending. The anti-globalisation movement opposes the neoliberal concern with the accumulation of wealth and exploitation of people and the planet, while also reflecting social work values of respect and social justice. Such factors, together with the re-engagement with a radical/critical practice, provide social work with 'resources for hope' (Batsleer and Humphries, 2000).

Radical/critical practice: theoretical considerations

As I have argued elsewhere (Rogowski, 2008), radical/critical practice draws on Marxist thought, with problems confronting people being seen as social and structural rather than individual in nature, and arising from class, 'race', gender and other forms of oppression. The focus is on political action and social change, while simultaneously addressing the immediate needs of individuals. It involves anti-racist/ sexist and anti-oppressive/discriminatory perspectives along with empowerment and advocacy (Payne, 2005b).

Put another way, 'pure' radical theory was based on class oppression during the 1970s (Bailey and Brake, 1975) and involved five themes (Langan and Lee, 1989). First, most problems experienced by clients were not the result of personal failings but instead were the result of living in a society dominated by inequality, oppression and class division. Second, casework was seen as a way of individualising what were essentially collective problems, this being both ineffective as well as pathologising. Third, there was an emphasis on collective approaches, of group and community work, in addressing issues of concern. Fourth, as we have already seen, 'professionalism' itself was critiqued because, through education and training, social workers were separated from users and the population at large. This suggested a different, more equal, kind of relationship with users in which the latter's knowledge and experience was valued. Finally, the ensuing analysis of society's ills was a socialist one that sees class as the main divide in society.

As discussed in Chapter Three, during the 1980s and into the 1990s, the focus on class oppression was complemented by other forms of oppression including those arising from 'race' and gender (Langan and Lee, 1989), as well as by by the critical theory of the Frankfurt School and by postmodern perspectives (Leonard, 1997; Fook, 2002). For instance, critical perspectives emerged in relation to feminism (Hanmer and Statham, 1999; Dominelli, 2002b), anti-racism (Dominelli, 1997) and anti-discriminatory/anti-oppressive practice (for example, Dalrymple and Burke, 1995; Dominelli, 2002a, 2009b; Thompson, 2006). At one level, such changes are to be welcomed because, influenced by various users movements, they highlight the discrimination faced by not only women and black people but also by older people and those with disabilities and mental health problems. However, at another level, as feminism's paradigm shift indicates (see Chapter One), whereas commonality provided a basis for joint, collective action, the 1990s stress on women's identity led to a fragmentation that is part and parcel of neoliberal policies that in turn accentuate the belief in individualism. Importantly, this new emphasis on identity also led to a retreat from class analysis and politics, together with the possibility these offer for collective action. It also meant sidelining issues of poverty and equality, which was seen as a major weakness leading to demands for a return to a 'politics of redistribution' (Fraser, 1997).

In practice, much of critical social work, at least in its broadest sense, sought to overcome fragmentation and make links between oppression and material inequality. What is more problematic is the extent to which the more extreme postmodern proponents of critical social work can actually do this. Returning to some of the points made in Chapter One, these include postmodernism's radical individualism, which rejects all bases of collective identity, its rejection of structural explanations of poverty and inequality, and its moral relativism, which amounts to nihilism (Ferguson, 2008, pp 115-18). A key failing of postmodernism is that it provides little in terms of practice or a theoretical framework for making links between individual or group or community work and wider structural processes. To give a current example, it is difficult to understand or effectively challenge the withering away of relationship-based social work without relating this to the context of the marketisation of social work and managerialism as a whole. Then again, if, following postmodernism, important policy themes are difference, diversity and choice, this can result in the neglect of inequality, increased privatisation and stricter regulation of the lives of some of the poorest groups in society. Furthermore, the Foucauldian emphasis on the local, the specific and the particular, reinforces and legitimises that neglect, with the failure to address the material realities that shape people's lives being a feature of postmodern or 'constructive' social work (Parton and O'Byrne, 2000). Finally, with regard to the charge of nihilism, this is evidenced by postmodernism's failure to specify mechanisms of change together with an inability to demonstrate why change is better than no change.

Following theorists such as Callinicos (1999), an acceptance of the postmodern scepticism of the 'false universalism' of the welfare state over Enlightenment's promise of universal emancipation admittedly presents a problem. However, the (limited) postmodern repost is that every universalism is seen as a masked particularism that excludes many, so one must then decide which particularism, or group of particularisms, one prefers. In terms of welfare policy, there are inherent dangers in such a view, especially when the idea of welfare itself is under threat. This is because it can allow governments wanting to cut expenditure to play groups off against each another as they argue over the limited resources on offer. It can also facilitate a backlash against oppressed groups where genuine demands for affirmative action can be portrayed as being at the expense of the basic welfare needs of the majority. The alternative answer to the failings of the Enlightenment project is to seek *genuine* universality, and by this I mean a social and political order in which *everyone* is included. It is a world where all humans, regardless of class, 'race', gender, age or impairment, can coexist on an equal basis, and where their needs will be met and their views valued. It is about a better world simply because it is impossible to envisage an inclusionary neoliberal/capitalist world (Oliver and Barnes, 1998).

A confederation of diversities

As always, creating a better world is always the hardest part of any emancipatory project. But there are challenges to neoliberalism in the form of the anti-globalisation movement and the current concern with happiness and well-being (Ferguson, 2008).

The 1990s saw left-wing politics dominated by concerns with identity and difference, often reflecting distrust between the various groups resisting different aspects of oppression and exploitation. However, what was significant in the anti-globalisation movement was its ability to bring together these disparate groups – trade unionists, environmentalists, peace campaigners, feminists, socialists and many others. It amounts to 'unity in diversity' (Leonard, 1997, p 177) and protests such as this could arguably lead to the establishment of a new kind of political party, one where member organisations join together not to obliterate their separate identities, but to express them in part through solidarity. Such a party could be described as a 'confederation of diversities'.

Being involved politically may be all well and good, but what about scope for a radical social work practice? As always, radical social work has always been stronger on theory than practice, especially so given the demise of group and community work as part and parcel of social work. Even so, social workers can pursue 'radical ideas in practice ... in their individual work with service users, through the relationships they build with them, the attention they pay to their needs and rights and in their own personal recognition of the oppression and discrimination they face' (Ferguson and Woodward, 2009, p 75). Examples of this admittedly more restricted view of radical practice are given later in this chapter, but at this stage it is worth elaborating on the current concern with happiness and well-being. This is something that Ferguson comments on and that is a major theme of Bill Jordan's work in his efforts to reinvigorate social work.

Social work, welfare and well-being

Like many others, Jordan (2007, 2008, 2010) has never been comfortable with the narrow market mentality of neoliberalism. Drawing on developments in Europe, North America and Australasia, his essential argument is that we are living on the cusp of a cultural transformation. This entails a move from societies organised around economic growth and material consumption to those focusing on well-being and sustainability. This challenges the assumption that happiness is affected more by people's material circumstances than by their physical and mental health and their relationship with others. He highlights the significance of personal relationships, and the trust and participation needed to sustain a decent quality of life, despite the dominance of the economic model, particularly its neoliberal form, which remains the major basis for political and social institutions and policy. As a result, well-being should be seen and accepted in terms of its social value and be incorporated into policy decisions. As he puts it, 'what hurts about being poor is not so much the absence of comforts and luxuries, but the stigma of official surveillance, the contempt of mainstream citizens, the exclusion from civil associations, and the damage to personal relations'. As a result of this 'survival strategies are stressful because they have to be pursued against the current of society's complacent assumptions about its own integrity and deservingness' Jordan (2007, pp vi-vii).

What is surprising is that it is a professor of economics at the London School of Economics, namely Richard Layard, rather than a psychologist whose work has been influential in the well-being debate. Layard (2005, p i) calls for a new approach to public policy that promotes the common good and for 'a shift to a new perspective where people's feelings are paramount'. What becomes clear is that the promise of neoliberalism has not been fulfilled, despite its claims that the 'trickle-down' of wealth would result not only in a wealthier society but also a better one, with happier and more contented citizens/consumers. He concludes that although 'Western societies have got richer, their people have become no happier.... Despite all the efforts ... human happiness has not been improved' (Layard, 2005, pp 3-4). The UNICEF (2007) report noting the unhappiness of children in the UK certainly endorses this point. The fact is that the consumerist society has not only failed to bring greater happiness, but has also led to greater levels of mental illness (CEPMHPG, 2006). Happiness, well-being and overall quality of life, rather than increased material consumption, should therefore be the goal.

For Jordan (2007), this analysis provides an opportunity to reassert the value of social work. This involves eschewing the views of accountants, managers and government ministers, instead re-emphasising social work concerns with relationships and feelings. These should not be regarded as vague, 'woolly' concepts, even at a time such as this when social work is preoccupied with (often so-called) evidence-based practice. In fact, evidence-based practice has often tied social work or, more appropriately, has been forced to tie social work too closely to neoliberal agendas of the Thatcherite and

New Labour kind. This has meant an emphasis on individualism, choice and markets, with social work represented in terms of gains in independence, choice (and thus mobility) and economic functioning (Jordan, 2006), with personalisation being an example of this. The well-being agenda reflects a move away from such preoccupations to ones that are more in line with a future consisting of environmental awareness, a revival of respect and mutuality within ethnic diversity, and a vision of our collective quality of life. Jordan's latest work shows how the Third Way's combination of market-friendly, value-led principles has failed, and that in the wake of the economic crash, public policy is in search of a new moral compass (Jordan, 2010). It all resonates with social work concerns rather than with material consumption or the work ethic. For many, the current emphasis on individual consumption and the reliance on big business to deliver personal fulfilment are beginning to look out of place.

It could be argued that allegedly 'woolly' concepts such as relationships and feelings lead to a loss of intellectual and scientific rigour, but this is too simplistic. Social work cannot be satisfactorily represented in terms of gains in independence, choice and economic functioning; rather, it must also stress its value in the emotional, social and communal spheres of life Jordan (2007). The very fact that hard-nosed economists are trying to analyse such phenomena certainly provides an opportunity to give these dimensions of experience the same level of attention as the material spheres. The challenge for social workers, therefore, is to move themselves and users beyond concerns with material consumption and instrumental outcomes. In a culture of choice and self-expression, at the very least happiness and well-being demand a balance by way of emotional closeness, respect and collective solidarity, values that in turn connect to notions of social justice and diversity.

The interpersonal economy and social work

The value of social work is far more than the neoliberal preoccupation of being able to deliver services to individuals whose well-being is seen to lie in a choice of alternative suppliers or particular interventions to target specific behaviours. Such a preoccupation involves an emphasis on services packaged and delivered to encourage choice, on efficiency and effectiveness, and on commissioning under contract so as to allow costs to be accounted for and outcomes recorded. At best, this is a very narrow view of how to maximise well-being, implying as it does that services are one-off experiences that can be consumed one after another. It also overlooks the value generated by the 'interpersonal economy' and fails to recognise a number of issues (Jordan, 2007). First, social work involves interactions with users in which emotions such as empathy, trust and respect are involved, and it is these mechanisms of interpersonal economy that produce much of the value of the very same social work/care services. Second, social workers often deal in long-term dependences, not one-off experiences, and social care itself is not simply about 'independence', but about people's quality of relationships in systems of relationships whereby people give and receive support over many years. Third, social care services create cultures and contexts in which professionals and users make sense of the world and experience it. Anti-discriminatory and anti-oppressive approaches come into play so that services are sensitive to gender and ethnic differences and create a diversity of understandings whereby groups are in dialogue about society and social interactions.

Furthermore, although individual autonomy and mobility are aspects of well-being that allow people to move between options, the disadvantage is that these are a questionable basis for the social relations of well-being. A situation where a significant amount of geographic mobility and changing of options leads to high levels of income and social inclusion in some areas and poverty and exclusion in others is not conducive to trust, cohesion and community participation (Jordan, 2006). Services that aim to provide a context for equal citizenship and social justice should be accessible for all and encourage interaction between different groups and communities.

Another point worth emphasising is that social work practice that focuses on protecting vulnerable individuals, facilitating behavioural change and meeting identified need is reconcilable with a concern with an individual's well-being. Statutory social work therefore does have a role if it responds by engaging with users' own understanding of their identities and the quality of their lives. By analysing problems and interventions in terms of the interpersonal economy it can, for example, reduce harmful emotions and actions while enhancing positive ones, improve relations with friends and neighbours, and even, if extended, lead to activism in a social movement (Jordan, 2007). Social work is also an element in the current concern with 'community' and 'cohesion' in that it shares many of the methods and values of community work, and to try to separate them, as New Labour has, is at best artificial.

Advocates of evidence-based practice would be hard pushed to find examples of improved outcomes in recent approaches to service delivery. One has only to recall the fact that there has been an increase in the numbers of children and young people with emotional and behavioural issues or mental health concerns, and that prisons and young offenders' institutions are fuller than ever. Moreover, greater material inequality has been accompanied by an increase in types of behaviour that can be linked to feelings of hopelessness and resistance, such as self-harm and anti-social behaviour. Technical, 'what works' fixes or tough law and order measures can hardly be said to have been a success, nor can seeing services as sequential one-off experiences, delivered in occasional packages, that can even be counterproductive. Take, for example, children and young people who need to be accommodated or have problems that require the help and support of a social worker; such cases should not be dealt with in a series of separate experiences. In the case of children who need to be accommodated, a fragmented approach can lead to frequent moves, often resulting in educational underachievement, drug use, offending and eventual homelessness. This could be remedied by creating social value through *positive* and *consistent* relationships and exchanges between adults, not least social workers, and children and young people.

Taken as a whole, a concern with happiness and well-being for all is at odds with a government that adheres 'to an incoherent version of social order, which jeopardises the very fabric of social reproduction' (Jordan, 2007, p 140). New Labour's overregulation of welfare, social relations and certain aspects of social work, to the extent that it has become a tool of oppression, has been a failure (Jordan, 2010) . During my lifetime, we have witnessed a move from a collectivist welfare state to a competitive individualist society where everyone takes responsibility for themselves. If, for whatever reason, individuals are unable to do this, they are dealt with in an increasingly authoritarian way. What has been lost in this process are collective measures for social protection, which have been sacrificed in order to achieve the goals of more flexible market-oriented systems and people. This may have helped the UK and other countries adapt to the demands of globalisation, but it has gone hand in hand with a diminution in qualities such as mutual respect, acceptance and consideration of others. There may be higher living standards for many, but in terms of well-being little has changed. Something certainly seems wrong. As Jordan (2007, p 127) succinctly puts it:

> The cult of self, and the culture of change, of adaption to the demands of the markets, does not give us the best possible quality of life, given our technological and organisational capabilities. There is something wrong in economics itself (or, as a Marxist might say, in the logic of capitalism) which limits the possibilities for improving our happiness. Well-being has stalled.

A mainstream social order based on self-responsibility, choice and moving between options looks increasingly unworkable, given the social problems – such as drug and alcohol misuse, poverty, crime, minority disaffection and so on – that afflict large sections of society. Social work's concern with, and involvement in, the interpersonal economy provides a more promising arena for ensuring social order in which diversity and freedom are reconciled with respect and belonging. It is perhaps overly optimistic to say so, but there may even be signs of change, with *Every Child Matters* (DfES, 2004) acknowledging that children should *enjoy* as well as achieve, with social workers and their education colleagues well placed in promoting a better quality of life in the various establishments provided by education and social care. Well-being has entered the public consciousness and social work can play a part in demanding and working for change so as to ensure more communal solutions to shared social issues.

A future for social work?

Whether it is utilising the space opened up by the death of Baby Peter, reclaiming social work or making the most of the opportunities provided by the current emphasis on happiness and well-being, what Garrett, Ferguson and Jordan have in common is a somewhat sanguine view of the future possibilities for social work, notwithstanding the difficulties.

Garrett is surely correct in much of his analysis and there are opportunities to challenge the neoliberal orthodoxy. However, perhaps he overstates these opportunities; in particular, I am not so sure about the possibility of an economic regime change as a result of the world economic crisis (see below). But there have been some positive outcomes from the Baby Peter tragedy, including many of the recommendations of the Social Work Task Force (2009) report. A college for social work, for instance, would give the profession a voice and it is gratifying that all three major political parties have accepted this. However, it is all too easy to get carried away with the idea of a college, especially given BASW's concern about government interference and whether such an institution would be truly independent. Furthermore, there are impending massive public expenditure cuts to consider, so one wonders if the college will ever come to pass.

Meanwhile, Ferguson is certainly correct to advocate the continued relevance of a radical/critical practice, even though the opportunities for this are *far more* restricted than they were. There are few, if any, possibilities for the group and community work of the past. Those radical/critical opportunities that do remain are small-scale and piecemeal, though important nonetheless. Take, for example, a Zimbabwean family with young children fleeing torture who do not have leave to stay in the UK and hence are not entitled to benefits. As unbelievable as it may seem, one approach may simply be to send the family back to Zimbabwe or place the children in local authority accommodation if they are not being fed and properly cared for. But an alternative, more radical, response might be to put the family in touch with groups and organisations that specialise in helping people in a similar predicament. This could entail having to engage directly, or perhaps even clandestinely, with a particular group or organisation,

181

which may involve pointing out the deficiencies in the social worker's own agency's response. That group/organisation could then arrange for a solicitor to be involved, who in turn could contact the social worker's hierarchy to arrange weekly financial help for necessities such as food and fuel until the family's immigration status and other practicalities have been resolved.

Another example could involve a teenage girl being assaulted by her mother who has mental health issues. A social worker completing an assessment in this case could stress the fact that the mother was in touch with mental health services but that they only tended to become involved when she reached crisis point. Making the point that a more proactive, and if necessary sufficiently funded, service would have lessened the likelihood of the assault occurring would help highlight service deficiencies and lead to improvements. Finally, 'old' radical/critical strategies of encouraging and/or helping users to write letters of complaint and to contact councillors or MPs about issues and concerns still retain their relevance. This is despite the fact that on one occasion when I helped users to do this, the MP simply wrote back saying he could not help because of his busy schedule and advised that they wait for the housing department to respond to their query.

Such examples highlight, and amount to, White's (2009) view of 'quiet challenges' and resistance to managerial discourses and practices. This resistance can take different forms. One can mystify or conceal knowledge of users in order to acquire resources, amounting to the manipulation of knowledge and information on their behalf. Even apparent cooperation with a social work task may conceal resistance; for example, one could delay paperwork or assessment plans so that managers are manipulated into taking a particular course of action. Ignoring, bending or reinterpreting rules and procedures also have a role to play.

Finally, as Jordan points out, it may be that the current concern with well-being resonates with, and provides some opportunities for, social work. As Ferguson (2008) notes, however, there are concerns about the way this debate has been taken forward by Layard (2005) and New Labour. Rather than concentrating on asking questions about the kind of society that gives rise to unhappiness, the emphasis is on using measures such as cognitive behavioural therapy to help those suffering the adverse effects of such a society. This will save money because when their problems are alleviated these people will no longer be claiming benefits. What is striking about this line of argument is the total neglect of the fact that inequality is linked to every type of mental health (Pilgrim and Rogers, 2002). Moreover, what also becomes clear is how congruent the themes outlined in relation to the new science of happiness are with New Labour's Third Way ideas and policies, and with neoliberalism more generally. Health is seen as an individual's responsibility, poverty and inequality are seen as irrelevant, and the notion of welfare dependency is rejected.

A key problem that confronts social work and severely hinders its future is that all three major parties in the UK, along with most of the governments and the main political parties in the developed (and increasingly the developing) world, accept a consensus that involves seeing neoliberalism (or, in more overtly Marxist terms, global capitalism) as the only way forward. This is despite the global recession of 2008-10. The immediate cause may have been the unbridled greed and reckless risk taking associated with the bankers in the US, but it soon spread to the rest of the world, affecting in particular one of its most ardent supporters of free markets, the UK. However, it is not just a case of simply blaming the bankers and the banking system; what occurred was a consequence of globalisation and global capitalism itself. The world's political leaders, led by Barack Obama and Gordon Brown, vowed that such a situation would not be allowed to be repeated and that fundamental reform and regulation of the world financial system was required. There have been many fine words and speeches at various meetings and conferences, including those of the current Conservative–Liberal Democrat coalition government, to this effect. But when one looks at what has actually happened, one is immediately struck by the fact that little, if anything, has changed. To the extent that something may be done, that some sort of regulation may take place, the overall effect will merely be to prop up the system that is the root of all the problems. To cut a long story short, the dominance of neoliberalism remains and the economic and political system this entails has emerged from the crisis largely unscathed. This is the reason why we have surely seen *both* the changing face of social work and arguably its fall.

In brief, the belief in free markets and limited state intervention remains intact and the resulting policies are affecting developments in social work and social care to the extent that they threaten the very existence of the profession. In such a situation, the future of social work remains uncertain and one is tempted to say that there is unlikely to be a return to what can be considered its heyday in the 1970s. It may be that we are witnessing the demise of what one Arab man in Morocco told me back then was a 'noble profession'. The caring and supportive side of state social work does not fit with neoliberal ideology that emphasises that people should take responsibility for their own lives, seeking support from family, friends, local community and voluntary organisations where necessary. Any element of 'care' may well be limited resulting in social workers becoming more like navigators, helping users choose what service they require, or even simply acting as the middleman/woman in an increasingly business-oriented enterprise, aiming to satisfy their customer's needs. To the extent that a more substantial role remains, it will emphasise the authoritarian, controlling aspects of present-day social work, something that has increasingly been in evidence over recent decades. It may also be the case that eventually social work will no longer be a unified profession as such. One has only to remember calls for separate degrees for those working with children and those working with adults in the wake of the Baby Peter case.

If social work does ceases to exist as a unified profession, there may be opportunities, characterised by less qualified support and care, for other workers to carry out what were social work responsibilities and roles. However, such workers will have less knowledge and understanding about the situations of the people they are dealing with and about their own position in the process of managing and controlling people who are essentially casualties of current societal arrangements. From its very beginnings, social work has attempted to challenge the status quo, and knowledge and understanding are required in order to do this. It is precisely because of this knowledge and understanding, gleaned from genuine attempts to develop a profession, that social work has been able to highlight inequalities and oppression in current neoliberal society. It is also because of this that social work has increasingly come under attack and, more recently under New Labour, been sidelined and largely ignored.

Perhaps all that can be expected over the coming years is that social workers will become even more the acceptable face of a state that offers no or minimal services. People will be expected to 'stand on their own feet', with social workers only intervening if people become a danger to themselves or others, and then only in an authoritarian way. As Dominelli (2009a, p 23) puts it, one scenario is that 'growing inequalities, housing shortages, rising food and fuel prices and the threat of unemployment can combine to confine social work interventions to the dustbin of history as irrelevant or parasitic'. That is, of course, unless practitioners find new responses and 'resources for hope' to both current and forthcoming challenges. Similarly, Cree (2009) points out that social work is at a crossroads and can either fight to hold on to its nascent professional status in the face of the encroachment of other professional groupings and managerialism or in effect retreat and accept the status quo. The reader will no doubt be aware which 'road' Garrett, Ferguson and Jordan advocate and towards which, perhaps surprisingly and a little hesitantly, I veer. Despite the many challenges and difficulties currently besetting social work, the opportunities that do remain need to be taken. This means acting collectively so as to ensure a stronger professional identity, as well as individually in one's own practice with users. If this is not done, the road will be left clear for those more concerned about maintaining the status quo than wanting a better, more just and equal world.

Conclusion

Some may find my narrative of the development of professional social work in the UK to the present day controversial. All would surely agree, however, that social work has changed and developed in response to changed political, economic, social and ideological circumstances, reaching its peak as the social democratic period was ending. It was a product of that era, a time of collectivism when the state, through the government of the day, played a key role in terms of ensuring that the needs of its people – through health, education, housing, employment, social security and social services – were met. Social workers provided the answer to social ills, both in terms of working directly with individuals, families, groups and communities, and in terms of arranging, advocating and coordinating the work of other agencies to meet needs. They possessed professional knowledge, understanding and skills, deploying these, at least to some extent, as they saw fit for the benefit of those they dealt with. Corresponding with an ideological move to the right, however, completed by the election of Thatcher, the situation changed.

The welfare state was transformed as a private sector ethos was injected into the delivery of public services, including improved targeting, cost-cutting measures and more 'consumer choice'. The selflessness of social workers and others, together with their ability to make effective use of public funds, was challenged by the view that citizens should approach welfare provision as they would a private consumer (Page, 2009a). By the end of the 1990s, the welfare state was no longer regarded as aiding social solidarity or redistribution; instead it was seen as a means to provide consumers with tailored, cost-effective services. Thatcherism succeeded 'in securing legitimation for the role of the market in the delivery of heartland social and welfare services, and in the role of management in securing cost effectiveness' (Ferguson et al, 2002, p 165).

New Labour embraced the new welfare culture, envisaging a modernised welfare state as having to work with the grain of market imperatives (Page, 2009b). No longer a social democratic party aiming to change society on egalitarian lines, it merely attempted to remove barriers to opportunity in the free market. This included the promotion of an active rather than a passive welfare state, the involvement of private and voluntary bodies, an emphasis on individuals advancing their own welfare and a concern with the quality and performance of services. Such themes will surely be developed and taken further by the Conservative–Liberal Democrat coalition. For social work, at the instigation of managers and politicians, the emphasis has, and will even more so be on 'getting more for less'. However, when it comes to this 'modernisation' of social work, the tensions, dilemmas and contradictions arising from *intensification* of work, the *individualisation* of users and the *inconvenience* of, albeit reduced, discretion will hopefully stubbornly remain (Harris and White, 2009b). A niche can be found for some progressive, even radical/critical, possibilities and as such social work does have a future.

Notes

[1] In April 2009, two young brothers aged 10 and 11 assaulted and tortured two other boys of a similar age in Edlington, South Yorkshire. The brothers subsequently received life sentences with a minimum sentence of five years in January 2010.

References

Adams (1996) *Social Work and Empowerment*, London: Macmillan.

Aldridge, M. (1994) *Making Social Work News*, London: Routledge.

Aldridge, M. and Eadie, T. (1997) 'Manufacturing an Issue: the case of probation officer training', *Critical Social Policy*, 17(1), pp 111-24.

Aldgate, J. and Statham, J. (2001) *The Children Act Now: messages from research*, London: Stationery Office.

Althusser, L. (1971) *Lenin, Philosophy and Other Essays*, London: New Left Books.

Apter, D. (1993) 'Social Democracy', in W. Outhwaite, T. Bottomore, E. Gellner, R. Nisbet and A. Touraine (eds) *Twentieth Century Social Thought*, Oxford: Blackwell.

Audit Commission (2002) *Integrated Services for Older People*, London: Audit Commission.

Audit Commission (2008) 'Every Child Matters: are we there yet?', Press Release, 29 October.

Bailey, R. and Brake, M. (eds) (1975) *Radical Social Work*, London: Edward Arnold.

Bamford, T. (1990) *The Future of Social Work*, London: Macmillan.

Barclay Report (1982) *Social Workers: their role and tasks*, London: Bedford Square Press.

Bardsley, L. (2009) 'Why I Had to Get Out of Home Care', *Community Care*, 22 October.

Barrett, M. and Philips, A. (eds) (1992) *Destabilising Theory: contemporary feminist debates*, Cambridge: Polity Press.

Barry, N. (1999) *Welfare*, Buckingham: Open University Press.

Batsleer, J. and Humphries, B. (eds) (2000) *Welfare, Exclusion and Political Agency*, London: Routledge.

Bauman, Z. (1991) *Modernity and Ambivalence*, Cambridge: Polity Press.

Bauman, Z. (1992) *Intimations of Modernity*, London: Routledge.

Bauman, Z. (1997) *Postmodernity and its Discontents*, Cambridge: Polity Press.

Beasley, C. (1999) *What is Feminism?*, London: Sage Publications.

Beck, U. (1992) *Risk Society*, London: Sage Publications.

Becker, H.S. (1963) *Outsiders: studies in the sociology of deviance*, London: Macmillan.

Bell, D. (1960) *The End of Ideology*, New York, NY: Free Press.

Bell, D. and Klein, R. (eds) (1996) *Radically Speaking: feminism reclaimed*, London: Zed Books.

Benhabib, S. (1992) *Situating the Self: gender, community and postmodernism in contemporary ethics*, Cambridge: Polity Press.

Beresford, P. and Croft, S. (1984) 'Welfare Pluralism: the new face of Fabianism', *Critical Social Policy*, 9.

Beresford, P. and Croft, S. (1993) *Citizen Involvement: a practical guide for change*, London: Macmillan.

Beresford, P. and Croft, S. (1995) 'Whose Empowerment? Equalising the competing discourses in community care', in R. Jack (ed) *Empowerment in Community Care*, London: Chapman and Hall.

Beresford, P. and Croft, S. (2004) 'Service Users and Practitioners Reunited: the key component for social work reform', *British Journal of Social Work*, 34(1), pp 53–68.

Beveridge, W. (1942) *Social Insurance and Allied Services* (Beveridge Report), London: HMSO.

Blagg, H. and Smith, D. (1989) *Crime, Penal Policy and Social Work*, Harlow: Longman.

Bottoms, A. (1995) 'The Philosophy and Politics of Punishment and Sentencing', in C. Clarkson and R. Morgan (eds) *The Politics of Sentencing Reform*, Oxford: Oxford University Press.

Bourdieu, P. (1984) *Distinction: a judgement of taste*, London: Routledge.

Bourdieu, P. (2001) *Acts of Resistance: against the new myths of our time*, Cambridge: Polity Press.

Bourdieu, P. et al (2002) *The Weight of the World: social suffering in contemporary society*, Cambridge: Polity Press.

Bowl, R. (2009) 'PQ Social Work Practice in Mental Health', in P. Higham (ed) *Post-qualifying Social Work Practice*, London: Sage Publications.

Brenner, N. and Theodore, N. (eds) (2002) *Spaces of Neo-liberalism*, Oxford: Blackwell.

Brewer, C. and Lait, J. (1980) *Can Social Work Survive?*, London: Temple Smith.

Brewster, R. (1992) 'The New Class? Managerialism and social work education and training', *Issues in Social Work Education*, 11(2), pp 81-93.

Broadhurst, K. and Hall, C. (2009) 'The Stuff You Can't Measure', *Professional Social Work*, July, pp 20-1.

Callinicos, A. (1999) *Social Theory: a historical introduction*, Cambridge: Polity Press.

Callinicos, A. (2001) *Against the Third Way*, Cambridge: Polity Press.

Callinicos, A. (2003) *An Anti-capitalist Manifesto*, Cambridge: Polity Press.

Cannan, C. (1994/95) 'Enterprise Culture, Professional Socialisation and Social Work Education in Britain', *Critical Social Policy*, 42, pp 5-18.

Carter, J. (ed) (1998) *Postmodernity and the Fragmentation of Welfare*, London: Routledge.

CCETSW (Central Council for Education and Training in Social Work) (1989) *Requirements and Regulations for the Diploma in Social Work*, Paper 30, London: CCETSW.

CEPMHPG (Centre for Economic Performance's Mental Health Policy Group) (2006) *The Depression Report: a new deal for depression and anxiety*, London: CEPMHPG, London School of Economics.

Charities Commission (2007) *Stand and Deliver: the future for charities delivering public services*, London: Charities Commission.

Charles, M. and Wilton, J. (2004) 'Creativity and Constraint in Child Welfare', in M. Lynbery and S. Butler (eds) *Social Work Ideals and Practice Realities*, Basingstoke: Palgrave Macmillan.

Charnley, H., Roddam, G. and Wiston, J. (2009) 'Working with Service Users and Carers', in R. Adams, L. Dominelli and M. Payne (eds) *Social Work: themes, issues and critical debates* (3rd edn), Basingstoke: Palgrave Macmillan.

Clarke, J. (1994) 'Capturing the Customer: consumerism and social welfare', Paper presented at ESRC Seminar 'Conceptualising Consumption Issues', Lancaster.

Clarke, J. (1996) 'After Social Work?', in N. Parton (ed) *Social Theory, Social Change and Social Work*, London: Routledge.

Clarke, J. (1998) 'Thriving on Chaos? Managerialism and social welfare', in J. Carter (ed) *Postmodernity and the Fragmentation of Welfare*, London:Routledge.

Clarke, J. (2004) *Changing Welfare, Changing States: new directions in social policy*, London: Sage Publications.

Clarke, J. (2005) 'New Labour's Citizens: activated, empowered, responsibilized, abandoned?', *Critical Social Policy*, 25(4), pp 447-63.

Clarke, J. and Cochrane, A. (1998) 'The Social Construction of Social Problems', in E. Saraga (ed) *Embodying the Social: constructions of difference*, London: Routledge.

Clarke, J. and Newman, J. (1997) *The Managerial State*, London: Sage Publications.

Commission on Social Justice (1994) *Social Justice: strategy for national renewal*, London:Vintage/IPPR.

Cooper, M. (1983) 'Community Social Work', in B. Jordan and N. Parton (eds) *The Political Dimensions of Social Work*, Oxford: Basil Blackwell.

Cree,V. (2009) 'The Changing Nature of Social Work', in R. Adams, L. Dominelli and M. Payne (eds) *Social Work: themes, issues and critical debates* (3rd edn), Basingstoke: Palgrave Macmillan.

Cree,V. and Myers, S. (2008) *Social Work: making a difference*, Bristol: The Policy Press.

Crook, S., Pakulski, J., and Waters, M. (1992) *Postmodernization: change in advanced society*, London: Sage Publications.

Dalrymple, J. and Burke, B. (1995) *Anti-Oppressive Practice: social care and the law*, Buckingham: Open University Press.

Davis, A. and Garrett, P.M. (2004) 'Progressive Practice for Tough Times: social work, poverty and division in the twenty-first century', in M. Lymbery and S. Butler (eds) *Social Work Ideals and Practice Realities*, Basingstoke: Palgrave Macmillan.

DCSF (Department for Children, Schools and Families) (2008) *Making It Happen: working together for children, young people and families*, London: DCSF.

DfES (Department for Education and Skills) (2004) *Every Child Matters: change for children*, London: Stationery Office.

DfES (2006) *Children's Workforce Strategy: building a world class workforce for children, young people and families*, London: Stationery Office.

DfES (2007) *Care Matters: time for a change*, London: DfES.

DH (Department of Health) (1988) *Protecting Children: a guide for social workers undertaking a comprehensive assessment*, London: HMSO.

DH (1989) *Caring for People*, London: HMSO.

DH (1995) *Child Protection: messages from research*, London: HMSO.

DH (1998) *Modernising Social Services: promoting independence, improving protection, raising standards*, London: Stationery Office.

DH (2002) *Requirements for Social Work Training*, London: DH.

DH (2010) *Building the National Care Service*, London: DoE.

DH/Department for Education and Employment/Home Office (2000) *Framework for the Assessment of Children in Need and their Families*, London: Stationery Office.

Dominelli, L. (1997) *Anti-racist Social Work* (2nd edn), Basingstoke: Palgrave Macmillan.

Dominelli, L. (2002a) *Anti-oppressive Social Work Theory and Practice*, Basingstoke: Palgrave Macmillan.

Dominelli, L. (2002b) *Feminist Social Work Theory and Practice*, Basingstoke: Palgrave Macmillan.

Dominelli, L. (2009a) 'Repositioning Social Work', in R. Adams, L. Dominelli and M. Payne (eds) *Social Work: themes, issues and critical debates* (3rd edn), Basingstoke: Palgrave Macmillan.

Dominelli, L. (2009b) 'Anti-oppressive Practice: the challenges of the twenty-first century', in R. Adams, L. Dominelli and M. Payne (eds) *Social Work: themes, issues and critical debates* (3rd edn), Basingstoke: Palgrave Macmillan.

Donzelot, J. (1979) *The Policing of Families*, London: Hutchinson.

Doyle, C. and Kennedy, S. (2009) 'Children, Young People, their Families and Carers', in P. Higham (ed) *Post-qualifying Social Work Practice*, London: Sage Publications.

Ely, P. and Denney, D. (1987) *Social Work in a Multi-racial Society*, Aldershot: Gower.

Engels, F. (2005 [1887]) *The Condition of the Working Class in England*, London: Penguin.

Eraut, M. (1994) *Developing Professional Knowledge and Competence*, London: Falmer Press.

Evans, T. (2009) 'Managing to be Professional? Team managers and practitioners in modernised social work', in J. Harris and V. White (eds) *Modernising Social Work: critical considerations*, Bristol: The Policy Press.

Farrington, D. and Langan, P. (1992) 'Changes in Crime and Punishment in England and America in the 1980s', *Justice Quarterly*, 9, pp 5-46.

Fell, P. and Hayes, D. (2007) *What Are They Doing Here? A critical guide to asylum and immigration*, Birmingham: Venture Press.

Ferguson, I. (2008) *Reclaiming Social Work: challenging neo-liberalism and promoting social justice*, London: Sage Publications.

Ferguson, I. and Woodward, R. (2009) *Radical Social Work in Practice: making a difference*, Bristol: The Policy Press.

Ferguson, I., Lavalette, M. and Mooney, G. (2002) *Rethinking Welfare*, London: Sage Publications.

Foley, P. and Rixon, A. (2008) *Changing Children's Services: working and learning together*, Bristol: The Policy Press.

Fook, J. (2002) *Social Work: critical theory and practice*, London: Sage Publications.

Foucault, M. (1977) *Discipline and Punish*, London: Allen Lane.

Fraser, D. (1973) *The Evolution of the British Welfare State*, London: Macmillan.

Fraser, N. (1997) *Justice Interruptus: critical reflections on the post-socialist condition*, London: Routledge.

Friedman, M. (1962) *Capitalism and Freedom*, Chicago, IL: University of Chicago Press.

Friedman, M. and Friedman, R. (1980) *Free to Choose*, London: Secker and Warburg.

Frost, N. (2005) *Child Welfare: major themes in health and social welfare*, London: Routledge.

Fukuyama, F. (1992) *The End of History and the Last Man*, London: Hamish Hamilton.

Garrett, P.M. (2002) 'Getting a Grip: New Labour and the reform of the law on child adoption', *Critical Social Policy*, 22(2), pp 174-202.

Garrett, P.M. (2003) *Remaking Social Work with Children and Families: a critical discussion on the 'modernisation' of social care*, London: Routledge.

Garrett, P.M. (2005) 'Social Work's Electronic Turn: notes on the deployment of information and communication technologies in social work with children and families', *Critical Social Policy*, 25(4), pp 529-53.

Garrett, P.M. (2009a) 'The Case of Baby P: opening up spaces for the debate on the "transformation" of children's services?', *Critical Social Policy*, 29(3), pp 533-47.

Garrett, P.M. (2009b) *'Transforming' Children's Services? Social work, neoliberalism and the 'modern' world*, Maidenhead: Open University Press.

Gelsthorpe, L. (1997) 'Feminism and Criminology', in M. Maguire, R. Morgan and R. Reiner (eds) *The Oxford Handbook of Criminology*, Oxford: Oxford University Press.

Gelsthorpe, L. and Morris, A. (1994) 'Juvenile Justice 1945-1992', in M. Maguire, R. Morgan and R. Reiner (eds) *The Oxford Handbook of Criminology*, Oxford: Oxford University Press.

General Social Care Council (2008) *Social Work at its Best: a statement of social work roles and tasks for the 21st century*, London: General Social Care Council.

George, V. and Wilding, P. (1976) *Ideology and Social Welfare*, London: Routledge and Kegan Paul.

George, V. and Wilding, P. (1994) *Welfare and Ideology*, London: Harvester Wheatsheaf.

Gibbins, J.R. (1998) 'Postmodernism, Post-structuralism and Social Policy', in J. Carter (ed) *Postmodernity and the Fragmentation of Welfare*, London: Routledge.

Giddens, A. (1994) *Beyond Left and Right*, Cambridge: Polity Press.

Giddens, A. (1998) *The Third Way*, Cambridge: Polity Press.

Giddens, A. (2000) *The Third Way and its Critics*, Cambridge: Polity Press.

Giddens, A. (ed) (2001) *The Global Third Way Debate*, Cambridge: Polity Press.

Goldson, B. (1999) *Youth Justice: contemporary policy and practice*, Aldershot: Ashgate.

Goldson, B. (2000) *The New Youth Justice*, Lyme Regis: Russell House.

Goldson, B. (2007) 'New Labour's Youth Justice: a critical assessment of the first two terms', in G. McIvor and P. Raynor (eds) *Developments in Social Work with Offenders*, London: Jessica Kingsley.

Goldson, B. and Muncie, J. (eds) (2006) *Youth Crime and Justice*, London: Sage Publications.

Gray, J. (1989) *Liberalisms: essays in political philosophy*, London: Routledge.

Green, D.G. (1979) *The New Right*, Hemel Hempstead: Harvester Wheatsheaf.

Green, J. (2009) 'The Deformation of Professional Formation: managerial targets and the undermining of professional judgement', *Ethics and Social Welfare*, 3(2), pp 115-30.

Griffiths, A.W., Griffith, J. and Jarrett, A. (2009) 'Social Work and Older People: a view from over Offa's Dyke', in P. Higham (ed) *Post-qualifying Social Work Practice*, London: Sage Publications.

Griffiths, R. (1983) *NHS Management Inquiry*, London: Department of Health.

Griffiths, R. (1988) *Community Care Agenda for Action*, London: Department of Health.

Hagell, A. and Newburn, T. (1994) *Persistent Young Offenders*, London: Policy Studies Institute.

Hall, C., Peckover, S. and White, S. (2008) 'How Practitioners Use ICT in Social Care Work', *Community Care*, 15 May, pp 26-7.

Hall, S. (1998) 'The Great Moving Nowhere Show', *Marxism Today*, November-December, pp 9-15.

Hall, S., Critcher, C., Jefferson, T. and Roberts, B. (1978) *Policing the Crisis: mugging the state and law and order*, London: Macmillan.

Halmos, P. (1965) *The Faith of the Counsellors*, London: Constable.

Hamilton, P. (1997) 'The Enlightenment and the Birth of Social Science', in S. Hall and B. Gieben (eds) *Formations of Modernity*, Cambridge: Polity Press.

Hanmer, J. and Statham, D. (1999 [1988]) *Women and Social Work: towards a more woman-centred practice*, Basingstoke: Macmillan.

Harman, C. (1984) *Explaining the Crisis: a Marxist reappraisal*, London: Bookmarks.

Harris, J. (1998) *Managing State Social Work: frontline management and the labour process perspective*, Aldershot: Ashgate.

Harris, J. (2003) *The Social Work Business*, London: Routledge.

Harris, J. (2004) 'Consumerism: social development or social delimitation?', *International Social Work*, 47(4), pp 533-42.

Harris, J. (2009) 'Customer-citizenship in Modernised Social Work', in J. Harris and V. White (eds) *Modernising Social Work: critical considerations*, Bristol: The Policy Press.

Harris, J. and White, V. (2009a) 'Introduction: modernising social work', in J. Harris and V. White (eds) *Modernising Social Work: critical considerations*, Bristol: The Policy Press.

Harris, J. and White, V. (2009b) 'Afterword: intensification, individualisation, inconvenience, interpellation', in J. Harris and V. White (eds) *Modernising Social Work: critical considerations*, Bristol: The Policy Press.

Harris, R. (1996) 'Telling Tales: probation in the contemporary social formation', in N. Parton (ed) *Social Theory, Social Change and Social Work*, London: Routledge.

Harvey, D. (2005) *A Brief History of Neo-liberalism*, Oxford: Oxford University Press.

Harvey, L. (1990) *Critical Social Research*, London: Hyman Unwin.

Hay, C. (1996) *Restating Social and Political Change*, Buckingham: Open University Press.

Hayek, F.A. (1960) *The Constitution of Liberty*, London: Routledge and Kegan Paul.

Hayek, F.A. (1982) *Law, Legislation and Liberty: a new statement of the principles of the liberal principles of justice and political economy, vols. 1-3*, London: Routledge and Kegan Paul.

Healy, K. and Meagher, G. (2004) 'The Reprofessionalization of Social Work: collaborative approaches for achieving professional recognition', *British Journal of Social Work*, 34(2), pp 243-60.

Higham, P. (2006) *Social Work: introducing professional practice*, London: Sage Publications.

Higham, P. (2009) *Post-qualifying Social Work Practice*, London: Sage Publications.

Hill-Collins, P. (1991) *Black Feminist Theory: knowledge, consciousness and the politics of employment*, London: Routledge.

Hills, J. and Stewart, K. (2005) (eds) *A More Equal Society? New Labour, poverty, inequality and exclusion*, Bristol: The Policy Press.

Holmes, R. (2008) *The Age of Wonder: how the Romantic generation discovered beauty and the terror of science*, London: Harper Press.

Home Office (1984) *Probation Service in England and Wales: statement of national objectives and priorities*, London: Home Office.

Home Office (1987) *Efficiency Scrutiny of Her Majesty's Probation Inspectorate*, London: Home Office.

Home Office (1988) *Punishment, Custody and the Community*, Cmnd 424, London: HMSO.

Home Office (1995) *New Arrangements for the Recruitment and Qualifying Training of Probation Officers*, London: Home Office.

Home Office/Department of Health/Department of Education and Science/Welsh Office (1991) *Working Together Under the Children Act 1989: a guide to arrangements for inter-agency co-operation for the protection of children from abuse*, London: HMSO.

Home Office/Department of Health (1992) *Memorandum of Good Practice on Video Recording with Child Witnesses for Criminal Proceedings*, London: HMSO.

Horner, N. (2009) 'Understanding Intervention', in R. Adams, L. Dominelli and M. Payne (eds) *Social Work: themes, issues and critical debates* (3rd edn), Basingstoke: Palgrave Macmillan.

Howe, D. (1991) 'Knowledge, Power and the Shape of Social Work Practice', in M. Davies (ed) *The Sociology of Social Work*, London: Routledge.

Howe, D. (1992) 'Child Abuse and the Bureaucratisation of Social Work', *Sociological Review*, 40(3), pp 491–508.

Howe, D. (2002) 'Relating Theory to Practice', in M. Davies (ed) *Companion to Social Work* (2nd edn), Oxford: Blackwell.

Hughes, L. and Owen, H. (eds) (2009) *Good Practice in Safeguarding Children: working effectively in child protection*, London: Jessica Kingsley.

Humphries, B. (2004) 'An Unacceptable Role for Social Work: implementing immigration policy', *British Journal of Social Work*, 34, pp 93–107.

Hunter, S. and Ritchie, P. (eds) (2007) *Co-production and Personalisation in Social Care: changing relationships in the provision of social care*, London: Jessica Kingsley.

IFSW (International Federation of Social Workers) (2000) 'Definition of Social Work', www.ifsw.org

Ivory, M. (2005) 'Knock it Down and Start Again', *Community Care*, 20-26 October, pp 32-4.

Johnson, T. (1993) 'Professions', in W. Outhwaite, T. Bottomore, E. Gellner, R. Nisbet and A. Touraine (eds) *Twentieth Century Social Thought*, Oxford: Blackwell.

Jones, C. (1996) 'Anti-intellectualism and the Peculiarities of British Social Work Education', in N. Parton (ed) *Social Theory, Social Change and Social Work*, London: Routledge.

Jones, C. (1999) 'Social Work: regulation and managerialism', in M. Exworthy and S. Halford (eds) *Professionalism and the New Managerialism in the Public Sector*, Buckingham: Open University Press.

Jones, C. (2004) 'The Neo-liberal Assault: voices from the frontline of British social work', in I. Ferguson, M. Lavalette and E. Whitemore (eds) *Globalisation, Global Justice and Social Work*, London: Routledge.

Jones, D. (1989) 'The Successful Revolution', *Community Care*, 30 March, pp 1-2.

Jones, D. (1993) 'The Successful Revolution in Juvenile Justice Continues: but for how long?', *Justice of the Peace*, 8 May, pp 297-8.

Jones, R. (2008) Letter in *Community Care*, 17 April, p 12.

Jordan, B. (2001) 'Tough Love: social work, social exclusion and the Third Way', *British Journal of Social Work*, 31, pp 527-46.

Jordan, B. (2006) *Social Policy for the Twenty-first Century: new perspectives, big issues*, Cambridge: Polity Press.

Jordan, B. (2007) *Social Work and Well-being*, Lyme Regis: Russell House.

Jordan, B. (2008) *Welfare and Well-being: social value in public policy*, Bristol: The Policy Press.

Jordan. B. (2010) *Why the Third Way Failed: economics, morality and public policy*, Bristol: The Policy Press.

Jordan, B. with Jordan, C. (2000) *Social Work and the Third Way*, London: Sage Publications.

Jordan, B. and Parton, N. (1983) 'Introduction', in B. Jordan and N. Parton (eds) *The Political Dimensions of Social Work*, Oxford: Basil Blackwell.

Joseph, J. (2006) *Marxism and Social Theory*, Basingstoke: Palgrave Macmillan.

Kerr, H. (1981) 'Labour's Social Policy 1974–79', *Critical Social Policy*, 1(1), pp 5–17.

Kilbrandon Report (1965) *Children and Young People in Scotland*, Edinburgh: HMSO.

Labour Party (1997) *New Labour: because Britain deserves better*, London: Labour Party.

Laing, R.D. (1965) *The Divided Self: an existential study in sanity and madness*, Harmondsworth: Penguin.

Laming, Lord (2003) *The Victoria Climbié Inquiry*, London: Stationery Office.

Langan, M. (1993) 'The Rise and Fall of Social Work', in J. Clarke (ed) *A Crisis in Care? Challenges to social work*, London: Sage Publications.

Langan, M. and Clarke, J. (1994) 'Restructuring Welfare: the British welfare regime in the 1980s', in A. Cochrane and J. Clarke (eds) *Comparing Welfare States*, London: Sage Publications.

Langan, M. and Lee, P. (eds) (1989) *Radical Social Work Today*, London: Unwin Hyman.

Layard, R. (2005) *Happiness: lessons from a new science*, London: Penguin.

Leeding, A.E. (1976) *Child Care Manual for Social Workers*, London: Butterworths.

Le Grand, J. (2007) *Consistent Care Matters: exploring the potential of social work practices*, London: Department for Education and Skills.

Le Grand, J. and Bartlett, W. (1993) *Quasi-markets and Social Policy*, Basingstoke: Macmillan.

Lemert, C. (1994) 'Post-structuralism and Sociology', in S. Seidman (ed) *The Postmodern Turn: new perspectives on social theory*, Cambridge: Cambridge University Press.

Leonard, P. (1997) *Postmodern Welfare: reconstructing an emancipatory project*, London: Sage Publications.

Lipset, S. (1963) *Political Man*, London: Heinemann.

Lishman, J. (2009) 'Personal and Professional Development', in R. Adams, L. Dominelli and M. Payne (eds) *Social Work: themes, issues and critical debates*, Basingstoke: Palgrave Macmillan.

Loader, B. and Burrows, R. (1994) 'Towards a Post-Fordist Welfare State', in R. Burrows and B. Loader (eds) *Towards a Post-Fordist Welfare State*, London: Routledge.

London Edinburgh Weekend Return Group (1980) *In and Against the State*, London: Pluto Press.

Lopez, J. and Potter, G. (eds) (2001) *After Postmodernism: an introduction to critical realism*, London: Athlone.

Lowman, A. (2009) Letter in *Community Care*, 28 May, p 12.

Lymbery, M. (2004a) 'Responding to Crisis: the changing nature of welfare organisations', in M. Lymbery and S. Butler (eds) *Social Work Ideals and Practice Realities*, Basingstoke: Palgrave Macmillan.

Lymbery, M. (2004b) 'Managerialism and Care Management Practice with Older People', in M. Lymbery and S. Butler (eds) *Social Work Ideals and Practice Realities*, Basingstoke: Palgrave Macmillan.

Lymbery, M. (2010) 'A New Vision for Adult Social Care: continuities and change in the care of older people', *Critical Social Policy*, 30(1), pp 5-26.

Lymbery, M. and Butler, S. (2004) 'Social Work Ideals and Practice Realities: an introduction', in M. Lymbery and S. Butler (eds) *Social Work Ideals and Practice Realities*, Basingstoke: Palgrave Macmillan.

Lyon, D. (2000) 'Postmodernity', in G. Browning, A. Halcli and F. Webster (eds) *Understanding Contemporary Society*, London: Sage Publications.

Lyotard, F. (1986) *The Postmodern Condition*, Manchester: Manchester University Press,

MacDonald, C. (2006) *Challenging Social Work: the context of practice*, Basingstoke: Palgrave Macmillan.

Marcuse, H. (1964) *One Dimensional Man*, London: Routledge and Kegan Paul.

Marshall, T.H. (1996 [1950] *Citizenship and Social Class*, London: Pluto.

Martinson, R. (1974) 'What Works? Questions and answers about prison reform', *The Public Interest*, 35, pp 22-54.

Marx, K. (1970) *Marx and Engels Selected Works*, London: Lawrence and Wishart.

Marx, K. and Engels, F. (1996 [1848]) *The Manifesto of the Communist Party*, London: Pheonix.

McIvor, G. and Raynor, P. (eds) (2007) *Developments in Social Work with Offenders*, London: Jessica Kingsley.

—

McLaughlin, K. (2008) *Social Work, Politics and Society*, Bristol: The Policy Press.

Miliband, R. (1973) *The State in Capitalist Society*, London: Quartet Books.

Millie, A. (ed) (2009) *Securing Respect: behavioural expectations and anti-social behaviour in the UK*, Bristol: The Policy Press.

Mooney, G. and Law, A. (eds) (2007) *New Labour/Hard Labour: restructuring and resistance inside the welfare industry*, Bristol: The Policy Press.

Mullender, A. (1989/90) 'Groupwork as a Response to a Structural Analysis of Child Abuse', *Children and Society*, 3(4), pp 345-62.

Mullender, A. and Ward, D. (1991) *Self-directed Groupwork: users taking action for empowerment*, London: Whiting and Birch.

Muncie, J. (1999) *Youth and Crime: a critical introduction*, London: Sage Publications.

Newman, J. and Clark, J. (1994) 'Going About Our Business? The managerialisation of public services', in J. Clarke, A. Cochrane and E. McLaughlin (eds) *Managing Social Policy*, London: Sage Publications.

O'Brien, M. and Penna, S. (1998) *Theorising Welfare: Enlightenment and modern society*, London: Sage Publications.

Ofsted/Healthcare Commission/HM Inspectorate of Constabulary (2008) 'Joint Area Review: Haringey Children's Services Authority Area', www.ofsted.gov.uk/oxcare_providers/la_download/(id)/4657/(as)/JAR/jar_2008_309_Fr.pdf

Oliver, M. (2004) 'The Social Model in Action: if I had a hammer', in C. Barnes and G. Mercer (eds) *Implementing the Social Model of Disability: theory and research*, Leeds: The Disability Press.

Oliver, M. and Barnes, C. (1998) *Disabled People and Social Policy: from exclusion to inclusion*, London: Longman.

Orme, J., MacIntyre, G., Green Lister, P., Cavanagh, K. Crisp, B.R., Hussein, S., Manthorpe, J., Moriarty, J., Sharpe, E. and Stevens, M. (2009) 'What (a) Difference a Degree Makes: the evaluation of the new social work degree in England', *British Journal of Social Work*, 31(1), pp 161-78.

Otway, O. (1996) 'Social work with Children and Families: from child welfare to child protection', in N. Parton (ed) *Social Theory, Social Change and Social Work*, London: Routledge.

Page, R. (2009a) 'Conservative Governments and the Welfare State since 1945', in H. Bochel, C. Bochel, R. Page and R. Sykes (eds) *Social Policy: themes, issues and debates* (2nd edn), Harlow: Pearson Longman.

Page, R. (2009b) 'Labour Governments and the Welfare State since 1945', in H. Bochel, C. Bochel, R. Page and R. Sykes (eds) *Social Policy: themes, issues and debates* (2nd edn), Harlow: Pearson Longman.

Parton, N. (1985) *The Politics of Child Abuse*, London: Macmillan.

Parton, N. (ed) (1996a) *Social Theory, Social Change and Social Work*, London: Routledge.

Parton, N. (1996b) 'Social Theory, Social Change and Social Work: an introduction', in N. Parton (ed) *Social Theory, Social Change and Social Work*, London: Routledge.

Parton, N. (1996c) 'Social Work, Risk and the Blaming System', in N. Parton (ed) *Social Theory, Social Change and Social Work*, London: Routledge.

Parton, N. and O'Byrne, P. (2000) *Constructive Social Work: towards a new practice*, London: Palgrave Macmillan.

Payne, M. (2000) 'The Politics of Case Management and Social Work', *International Journal of Social Work*, 9(2), pp 82-91.

Payne, M. (2005a) *The Origins of Social Work: continuity and change*, Basingstoke: Palgrave Macmillan.

Payne, M. (2005b) *Modern Social Work Theory*, Basingstoke: Palgrave Macmillan.

Payne, M. (2009) *Social Care Practice in Context*, Basingstoke: Palgrave Macmillan.

Pearson, G. (1975) *The Deviant Imagination*, London: Macmillan.

Philips, J. (1996) 'The Future of Social Work with Older People in a Changing World', in N. Parton (ed) *Social Theory, Social Change and Social Work*, London: Routledge.

Pierson, J. (2010) *Tackling Social Exclusion* (2nd edn), Abingdon: Routledge.

Pilgrim, D. and Rogers, A. (2002) *Mental Health and Inequality*, London: Palgrave Macmillan.

Pitts, J. (1988) *The Politics of Juvenile Crime*, London: Sage Publications.

Pitts, J. (2001) 'Korrectional Karaoke: New Labour and the 'zombification' of youth justice', *Youth Justice*, 1(2), pp 3-12.

Pollock, A. (2004) *NHS Plc: the privatisation of our health care*, London: Verso.

Postle, K. (2001) 'The Social Side is Disappearing: I guess it started with us being called care managers', *Practice: social work in action*, 13(1), pp 13-26.

Powell, F. (2001) *The Politics of Social Work*, London: Sage Publications.

Powell, M. (1999) *New Labour, New Welfare State?*, Bristol: The Policy Press.

Powell, M. (2000) 'New Labour and the Third Way in the British Welfare State: a new and distinctive approach?', *Critical Social Policy*, 20(1), pp 39-60.

Pritchard, C. and Williams, R. (2010) 'Comparing Possible Child Abuse Related Deaths in England and Wales with the Major Developed Countries 1974-2006', *British Journal of Social Work*, 20:2.

Richmond, M. (1917) *Social Diagnosis*, New York, NY: Russell Sage.

Respect Task Force (2006) *Respect Action Plan*, London: Home Office.

Robinson, A. (2006) 'Towards an Intellectual Reformation: the critique of common sense and the forgotten revolutionary project of Gramscian theory', in A. Bieler and A. Morton (eds) *Images of Gramsci*, London: Routledge.

Rogowski, S. (1977) 'Consensus or Conflict?', *Social Work Today*, 8(23).

Rogowski, S. (1982) 'Managing the Heavy End: the way forward for IT', *Youth in Society*, 62, pp 10-12.

Rogowski, S. (1985) 'Intermediate Treatment: a critical appraisal', *Youth and Policy*, 12, pp 21-6.

Rogowski, S. (1990a) 'Radical Intermediate Treatment: some views from the field', *Youth and Policy*, 29, pp 20-8.

Rogowski, S. (1990b) 'Intermediate Treatment: towards a radical practice', *Youth and Policy*, 31, pp 30-5.

Rogowski, S. (1995) 'Youth Crime and Community-based Initiatives: a critical look at their development and some thoughts on a radical practice', *Practice: Social Work in Action*, 7(4), pp 43-52.

Rogowski, S. (2000/01) 'Young Offenders: their experience of offending and the youth justice system', *Youth and Policy*, 70, pp 52-70.

Rogowski, S. (2002) 'W(h)ither Social Work', *Professional Social Work*, March, p 7.

Rogowski, S. (2003/2004) 'Young Offenders: towards a radical/ critical social work practice', *Youth and Policy*, 82, pp 60-73.

Rogowki, S. (2006) 'The Lives, Views and Experiences of Three "Typical" Young Offenders', *Youth and Policy*, 91, pp 41-57.

Rogowski, S. (2007) 'Our Eroding Profession', *Professional Social Work*, March, pp 14-15.

Rogowski, S. (2008) 'Social Work with Children and Families: towards a radical/ critical practice', *Practice: Social Work in Action*, 20(1), pp 17-28.

Rogowski, S. (2009) 'A Twin Track to Trouble', *Professional Social Work*, June, pp 26-7.

Rogowski, S. (2010) 'Young Offenders: towards a radical/critical social policy', *Journal of Youth Studies*, 13(2), pp 197-211.

Rogowski, S. and Harrison, L. (1992) 'Community Social Work with Children and Families: a positive step forward', *Applied Community Studies*, 1(3), pp 4-20.

Rogowski, S., Harrison, L. and Limmer, M. (1989) 'Success with Glue Sniffers', *Social Work Today*, 21(9), pp 12-13.

Rogowski, S. and McGrath, M. (1986) 'United We Stand Up to Pressures that Lead to Child Abuse', *Social Work Today*, 17(37), pp 13-14.

Rose, N. (2000) 'Government and Control', *British Journal of Criminology*, 40, pp 321-39.

Rose, W. and Aldgate, J. (2000) 'Knowledge Underpinning the Assessment Framework', in *Assessing Children in Need and their Families: practice guidance*, Department of Health, London: Stationery Office.

Sapey, B. (2009) 'Engaging with the Social Model of Disability', in P. Higham (ed) *Post-qualifying Social Work Practice*, London: Sage Publications.

Sarup, M. (1993) *Poststructuralism and Postmodernism*, London: Harvester Wheatsheaf.

Schon, D. (1996) *Educating the Reflective Practitioner: towards a new design for teaching and learning in the professions*, San Francisco, CA: Jossey Bass.

Schur, E. (1973) *Radical Non-intervention: rethinking the delinquency problem*, Englewood Cliffs, NJ: Prentice Hall.

Schwarzmantel, J. (2008) *Ideology and Politics*, London: Sage Publications.

Scourfield, P. (2005) 'Implementing the Community Care (Direct Payments) Act: will the supply of personal assistants meet the demand and at what price?', *Journal of Social Policy*, 34(3), pp 469-88.

Scourfield, P. (2007) 'Are there Reasons to be Worried about the "Caretelization" of Residential Care?', *Critical Social Policy*, 27(2), pp 155-80.

Secretary of State for Social Services (1974) *Report of the Inquiry into the Care and Supervision Provided in Relation to Maria Colwell*, London: HMSO.

Secretary of State for Social Services (1988) *Report of the Inquiry into Child Abuse in Cleveland*, Cmnd 412, London: HMSO.

Seebohm Report (1968) *Report of the Committee on Local Authority and Allied Social Services*, Cmnd 2703, London: HMSO.

Simpkin, M. (1983) *Trapped Within Welfare* (2nd edn), Basingstoke: Macmillan.

Smart, B. (1993) *Postmodernity*, London: Routledge.

Smith, D. (ed) (2004) *Social Work and Evidence-based Practice*, London: Jessica Kingsley.

Smith, M. (1965) *Professional Education for Social Work in Britain*, Allen and Unwin cited in Younghusband, E. (1981) *The Newest Profession: a short history of social work*, Sutton: IPC Business Press.

Smith, R. (2007) *Youth Justice: ideas, policy and practice*, Cullompton: Willan.

Smith, R. (2008) *Social Work with Young People*, Cambridge: Polity Press.

Social Work Task Force (2009) *Building a Safe, Confident Future*, London: General Social Care Council.

Souhami, A. (2007) *Transforming Youth Justice: occupational identity and cultural change*, Cullompton: Willan.

Spandler, H. (2004) 'Friend or Foe? Towards a critical assessment of direct payments', *Critical Social Policy*, 24(2), pp 187-209.

Spencer, H. (1940 [1884]) *The Man Versus the State*, London: Watt.

Squires, S. (ed) (2008) *ASBO Nation: the criminalisation of nuisance*, Bristol: The Policy Press.

Stephenson, M., Giller, H. and Brown, S. (2007) *Effective Practice in Youth Justice*, Cullompton: Willan.

Stepney, P. (2006) 'Mission Impossible? Critical practice in social work', *British Journal of Social Work*, 36(8), pp 1289-307.

Stewart, J., Smith, P., Stewart, G. and Fullwood, C. (1994) *Understanding Offending Behaviour*, Harlow: Longman.

Sturges, P. (1996) 'Care Management and Practice: lessons from the USA', in C. Clark and I. Lapsey (eds) *Planning and Costing Care in the Community*, London: Jessica Kingsley.

Taylor, I., Walton, P. and Young, J. (1973) *The New Criminology: for a social theory of deviance*, London: Routledge and Kegan Paul.

Taylor-Gooby, P. (1981) 'The New Right and Social Policy', *Critical Social Policy*, 1(1), pp 18-31.

Taylor-Gooby, P. (2000) 'Blair's Scars', *Critical Social Policy*, 20(3), pp 331-48.

Thompson, J.B. (1990) *Ideology and Modern Culture*, Cambridge: Polity Press.

Thompson, N. (2002) 'Social movements, Social Justice and Social Work', *British Journal of Social Work*, 32(6), pp 711-22.

Thompson, N. (2006) *Anti-discriminatory Practice* (4th edn), London: Palgrave Macmillan.

Thorpe, D., Smith, D., Greenwood, C. and Paley, J. (1980) *Out of Care: the community support of juvenile offenders*, London: Allen and Unwin.

Tierney, J. (1996) *Criminology: theory and context*, Hemel Hempstead: Prentice Hall/Harvester Wheatsheaf.

Timmins, N. (1996) *The Five Giants: a biography of the welfare state*, London: Harper Collins.

Titmuss, R.M. (1950) *Problems of Social Policy*, London: HMSO.

Tong, R. (1989) *Feminist Thought*, London: Unwin Hyman.

TOPSS (Training Organisation for the Personal Social Services [now Skills for Care]) (2002) *The National Occupational Standards for Social Work*, Leeds: TOPSS.

Touraine, A. (1995) *Critique of Modernity*, Oxford: Blackwell.

Ungerson, C. (2004) 'Whose Empowerment and Independence? A cross-national perspective on 'cash for care' schemes', *Aging and Society*, 24(2), pp 189-212.

UNICEF (2007) *Report Card 7: Child Poverty in Perspective: an overview of child well-being in rich countries*, Florence: UNICEF Innocenti Research Centre.

Unison (2009) 'Shocking Social Work Survey Shows Child Protection is "Ticking Time Bomb"', Press Release, 26 January.

Vincent, J. (1983) 'Social Work as Ideology Experienced', in B. Jordan and N. Parton (eds) *The Political Dimensions of Social Work*, Oxford: Blackwell.

Wade, R. (2008) 'Financial Regime Change', *New Left Review*, 53, pp 5-23.

Webb, D. (1996) 'Regulation for Radicals: the state, CCETSW and the academy', in N. Parton (ed) *Social Theory, Social Change and Social Work*, London: Routledge.

Webb, S.A. (2006) *Social Work in a Risk Society: social and political perspectives*, London: Palgrave.

White, V. (2009) 'Quiet Challenges: professional practice in modernised social work', in J. Harris and V. White (eds) *Modernising Social Work: critical considerations*, Bristol: The Policy Press.

Whyte, B. (2009) *Youth Justice in Practice: making a difference*, Bristol: The Policy Press.

Williams, F. (1996) 'Postmodernism, Feminism and the Question of Difference', in N. Parton (ed) *Social Theory, Social Change and Social Work*, London: Routledge.

Wolf, N. (1993) *Fire with Fire: the new female power and how it will change the 21st century*, London: Chatto and Windus.

Woodroofe, K. (1962) *From Charity to Social Work*, London: Routledge.

Wootton, B. (1959) *Social Science and Social Pathology*, London: Allen and Unwin.

Young, J. (2007) *The Vertigo of Late Modernity*, London: Sage Publications.

Younghusband, E. (1981) *The Newest Profession: a short history of social work*, Sutton: IPC Business Press.

INDEX

Page references for notes are followed by

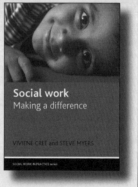